# Easy on the Helm

BOAT HANDLING UNDER SAIL AND POWER

# *Easy*

## BOAT HANDLING

# *on the Helm*

## UNDER SAIL AND POWER

### Tom Cunliffe

Illustrated by Tony Garrett

W · W · NORTON & COMPANY

New York    London

Copyright © 1992 by Tom Cunliffe

Illustrations © 1992 by Tony Garrett

All rights reserved.

Printed in the United States of America.

The text of this book is composed in Sabon,
with display type set in Baskerville Italic.
Composition by University Graphics, Inc.
Manufacturing by Maple-Vail Book Group.

Book design by Jack Meserole.

First Edition

Library of Congress Cataloging in Publication Data
Cunliffe, Tom.
    Easy on the helm : boat handling under sail and power Tom /
  Cunliffe ; illustrated by Tony Garrett.
        p.    cm.
    1. Boats and boating.      I. Title.
  GV775.C76    1992
  797.1—dc20
    ISBN 0-393-02851-8                                    89-26632

W.W. Norton & Company, Inc., 500 Fifth Avenue, New York, N.Y. 10110

W.W. Norton & Company Ltd., 10 Coptic Street, London WC1A 1PU

1 2 3 4 5 6 7 8 9 0

# CONTENTS

# LIST OF ILLUSTRATIONS

# INTRODUCTION

As the title suggests, this book is all about boat handling: at high and low speeds, under power or sail, in tight corners or in open water, in fair weather and in foul. It is not a sailing primer, and no attempt is made to explain the basic points of sailing. It has been written for those yachtsmen who have been on the water long enough to know what is happening most of the time, and who have learned enough to realize where their own shortcomings may lie.

In the pages that follow, the business of how a boat behaves in the water and why she does what she does will be examined in some detail. The theory and practice of sailing and sail handling will be discussed so as to help you sail more quickly, more easily, more safely, and have more fun in the process.

Understanding how a yacht handles under sail is the best possible training for dealing with her under power, and once the essentials of "sail control" have been covered, the book moves into this vital area. Maneuvering under sail is considered by some to be an advanced form of boat handling, but this is a misconception brought upon us by our machine-oriented society. In fact, the only thing a propeller can do that sails cannot guarantee on every occasion, is to "apply the brakes." Even then, the boat will often pull up unreliably, behaving like a road vehicle with an oil spillage over the starboard forward brake pads.

The secrets of successful handling vary for different boats under different conditions, but once the general principles have been understood and put into thoughtful operation, a skipper can have confidence under all circumstances. Boat handlers are not born, they are made. More specifically, they make themselves. The competent seaman depends on broad experience founded upon knowledge. The former part of the package is not for sale, though it can be partially substituted by structured exercises, but the knowledge is there for the taking. This book is designed to make it readily available so that you can fully evaluate the experience you have already acquired, and make every future maneuver count positively towards the rapid achievement of real expertise.

Tom Cunliffe

# Easy on the Helm

BOAT HANDLING UNDER SAIL AND POWER

# 1
## THE DYNAMIC BALANCING ACT: KEELS, RUDDERS, AND SAIL BALANCE

The sole arbiter of direction for a motor vehicle is the steering wheel. Where the front wheels are pointing, there it will go, unless it is a rally car operating in thick snow.

The skipper of a boat under either power or sail is faced with more subtle possibilities. In theory, when the tiller is pushed to starboard the yacht's head will swing easily to port, but this only works in practice so long as all the other forces acting upon her agree to let it be so. The reality rarely measures up to the ideal.

A boat will frequently show little interest in going where she is asked by a skipper whose only instrument of command is the helm, particularly when under sail at very low speeds or when starting from a standstill. For example, almost any sailing yacht will turn into the wind if the helm is released when she is moving through the water at a rate of knots, though the rapidity with which it happens depends on how she is being sailed. When a boat under power is stopped in a strong crosswind, her head will normally "blow off." If the operator wants her to turn her bow to windward, it may well not be enough to push the helm down and order "Slow ahead." If she refuses to answer, the solution will not lie in movements of the wheel or tiller alone. The only way of achieving the desired result will be to give her more power than would otherwise seem necessary.

These effects and a multitude of others are inherent in every boat afloat. Boats differ from one another in the details of their behavior, but the principles of turning and balance are the same for all of them.

# Keels

### CENTER OF LATERAL RESISTANCE

One of the most important concepts for the sailor to grasp is that when the rudder is turned in order to alter the boat's heading, she swivels around some central pivot point. The stern swings one way, the bow swings the other, and somewhere amidships is a particular spot which, in relative terms, does not move at all.

This swiveling effect is more noticeable when a boat is moving slowly. As her speed picks up, it will be increasingly difficult to discern, but it is there nonetheless.

The point around which the boat pivots is called the *center of lateral resistance*. As its name suggests, this is situated at the focus of the vessel's immersed lateral plane, and it is invariably found somewhere in the keel, more or less amidships. Its exact whereabouts is unimportant in this context, however. What you need to know is

Centre of lateral resistance

Centre of lateral resistance

When the rudder is moved off the centreline of the boat, her stern swivels one way, and her bow the other.

The net effect is a course alteration.

that when you shove the helm over so that the boat turns to port, the stern is going to cartwheel around to starboard, and vice versa.

Because the center of lateral resistance is the nominal point at which resistance to leeway-producing forces is concentrated, any sideways thrust exerted on the forward part of a yacht will encourage her to turn away from the force. In turn, any effort exerted abaft the pivot point will induce her to head up. This concept is of considerable importance when you are balancing a rig for speed and comfort, and it is a vital element of all low-speed maneuvers, especially under sail.

## KEEL STALL

When a boat is underway, her keel is always moving through the water at a slight angle because she is making leeway; the effect of this is that the keel develops lift. This lift is assisted by the fact that the boat will be carrying just a touch of *weather helm*, resulting from her built-in tendency to turn into the wind. The helm being held to weather holds the rudder blade to leeward, which deflects the water flowing past it and helps the keel to work more efficiently.

None of this happens at less than a certain critical speed, below which the keel is considered to be *stalled*. Once the keel has stalled, the boat's rudder becomes far less effective, and the residual lateral resistance of the boat depends entirely on the area of her immersed profile. The *dynamic* lateral resistance generated by any keel that is moving ahead through the water is far more effective than the *static* lateral resistance of the same keel being pushed sideways when the boat is not underway. This variance affects boats to different extents, but is always crucial to the way they handle.

## DIFFERENT TYPES OF KEEL

Over the last fifty years, the shapes of keels have developed beyond recognition. When you are choosing a boat, there is now something available to ideally suit your needs, no matter what use you intend for her. Different keel profiles have a profound effect on how efficiently a boat sails, how she handles at high and low speeds, whether or not she is able to look after herself in heavy weather, and how easy her motion will be. The type of keel should be one of the primary considerations for any prospective boat owner. For any skipper, a knowledge of the different possibilities is the foundation on which he can anticipate the probable behavior of an unfamiliar yacht. While keel profiles come in an almost infinite variety, for the purposes of comparison it should be sufficient to consider the basic properties of the four specific types illustrated.

*Straight-Lined Suzie* is a boat of traditional form. Such a vessel will track wonderfully straight, and should be easy to steer at sea. She will also have, in all probability, a lovely, easy motion. Unfortunately, the long keel which gives her such desirable characteristics is not so dynamically efficient as some of the more modern forms. When she is sailing closehauled, she will almost certainly make more leeway than *Winifred Whizzer,* for example. To offset this, her large lateral area gives her high lateral resistance when her keel is stalled. This means that her options at sea in heavy weather (see Chapter 16) are more numerous than those of some other boats. It also makes her less prone to being blown off-line when approaching a dock in a strong crosswind. Her heavy displacement will help her in this as well, by supplying her with a good reserve of inertia to resist a gusty wind.

   *Straight-Lined Suzie* will have a larger turning circle than some of the other boats because the amount of area in the water forward and aft of the pivot point will resist her ability to swivel around. She is also likely to be difficult to steer when going astern.

*Capable Clarrie* represents a good working compromise. She has enough lateral area to grip the water tolerably at low speeds, but her keel is sufficiently refined to deliver a dynamic resistance to leeway that is more than adequate for a cruising yacht. Her cutaway forefoot and the long lever arm between rudder and pivot point promise sharp handling in harbor, but her ability to travel straight at sea may possibly be inferior to *Straight-Lined Suzie*'s. When making sternway, *Clarrie* will be less likely to become unmanageable by tripping

'Straight-Line Suzie', an *old-fashioned, heavy displacement yacht.*

'Capable Clarrie', *a moderate fin-and-skeg hull.*

'Winifred Whizzer', a *light, modern fast cruiser.*

'Bilge-keel Bertha', a *shoal draft cruiser.*

over the heel of her own keel than will *Suzie,* but her motion at sea will be noticeably inferior.

**Winifred Whizzer,** if she has a decent rig, promises to be the most close-winded of all these boats. Her deep, narrow keel delivers tremendous dynamic efficiency, as does her high-aspect-ratio spade rudder. But, with boats, as in life generally, there is no such thing as a free lunch. *Winifred's* lateral resistance diminishes to next to nothing as she slows to sub-stalling speeds. This, coupled with the low inertia of lighter displacement, makes docking in strong winds highly entertaining and can lead to a serious reduction in survival possibilities when she is caught short-handed by storm conditions offshore. The lightness of her rig, and her shallow immersed underbody combine with her lack of displacement to produce a vessel whose motion in a seaway will be extremely lively.

*Winifred's* large rudder serves her well when it comes to steering a straight course—but it needs to, because without it she has little inherent tracking stability, so that steering her in a seaway may be hard work.

Her almost complete lack of immersed lateral area other than her keel means that her ability to swivel about her pivot point is phenomenal. At moderate speeds she should turn in little more than her own length, and she will be a joy for a muscular individual to steer astern, all of which makes her an easy vessel to maneuver at close quarters—unless, of course, it is blowing hard.

**Bilge-Keeled Bertha.** It is difficult to generalize about bilge-keeled yachts, because they vary greatly in such vital departments as depth of hull and displacement. *Bertha* herself is a fairly deep-drafted example of the type, and so will have a reasonable grip on the water even after her keels have stalled. She will not perform notably well to windward, owing to her lack of dynamic efficiency, but she should be steady on the helm. Compared with *Winifred Whizzer,* her pivot point is ill-defined and she has considerable immersed lateral area over most of her length. This will make her rather slow to turn in harbors.

A "bilge-keeler" with a flatter floor and deeper keels will behave in quite a different manner from *Bertha,* but by applying the principles noted in the first three types of keel form, it should be possible to hazard a useful guess as to her likely behavior.

The same sensible projection must, of course, apply to yachts with centerboards.

## Mast Rake, Fore-and-Aft Trim, and Helm Balance

### TRIM

A yacht is intended to float "to her marks." If she has been well designed, the relationship of her sails to her center of lateral resistance will be correct when she is properly trimmed. The result will be a well-mannered vessel.

However, as the illustration shows, if the boat is trimmed "down by the head," the center of lateral resistance shifts farther forward. The stern of the boat will then blow off the wind more easily, a greater degree of weather helm will be needed to keep her sailing in

Trim, and the centre of lateral resistance

Correct trim.

Down by the head – CLR moves forward, boat develops weather helm.

Down by the stern – CLR moves aft. Weather helm diminishes, or may be replaced by lee helm.

Mast upright. Boat is carrying lee helm.

centre of effort

clr

Mast raked aft.

Centre of effort moves aft relative to centre of lateral resistance. More weather helm is the result.

a straight line, and a "hard-mouthed" boat is the outcome. The most effective way of restoring her to her sanity may well be the simple expedient of shifting some weight aft.

The converse is also true, but because not many people complain that their boats have too little weather helm, this generally goes unnoticed. A knowledge of the theory is sometimes useful, however. If a long downwind leg is anticipated in a yacht which shows a tendency to develop weather helm, the crew's workload can be eased noticeably by trimming her down by the stern for the duration of that part of the voyage.

A yacht with a swiveling centerboard has an adjustable center of lateral resistance. With the board right down, she realizes her full potential of lateral resistance, which is what she wants as she sails to windward. On a reach, she can bring the board up part of the way, which generally also has the effect of moving it aft. This shifts her lateral resistance accordingly and helps balance the helm on a point of sailing where some yachts need all the assistance they can get.

## MAST RAKE

Just as a boat's underbody has a center of lateral resistance, so her sails have a center of effort. The location of this will depend upon sail combination and sheeting angles, but if the designer has been successful, the center of effort will combine with the various other forces acting on the moving boat to produce just a touch of weather helm.

If you are not satisfied with the position of the center of effort on, say, a sloop, it can often be adjusted by altering the rake of the mast. Yachts with a high performance rating are equipped with an adjustable backstay so as to encourage crews to do this as a matter of course for different points of sailing. Sails generally balance best when the boat is closehauled, but a little weather helm helps a boat to windward, so the mast can be raked aft when the breeze is forward of the beam (hardening the backstay will also help to keep the jib luff tight); downwind, the less helm the better, so the spar is encouraged to stand upright once more.

## Heeling and Rolling Effects on Steering

When a sailing boat rolls, or heels, she experiences two entirely different forces, both of which affect her steering characteristics.

## HEELING

As a yacht heels away from the wind, the driving force of her rig moves outboard and away from her mid-line. Once the sails are off-center from the line of the boat's progress, they try to screw her around into the wind. The helmsman counters this tendency by applying weather helm (pulling the tiller to windward). As the boat heels further, this propensity for rounding up will increase at a steady rate, but in the case of a boat of moderate design it is unlikely to cause too much in the way of hard work, until the boat is so far over that the helmsman's mind becomes concentrated on other matters. How-

Effect of heeling on helm balance (rig)

Centre of effort of rig

Weather helm required to counteract heeled rig

ever, in the 1980s, a design trend has appeared which aggravates this effect.

Many modern sailing boats have achieved a large accommodation space by increasing their beam to a higher proportion of their waterline length than has formerly been the norm. In this context,

The asymmetrical shape of this heeled hull will generate substantial weather helm.

Effect of heeling on helm balance (hull)

the effect of such beam on the comparatively flat-floored yachts in which it is often found, is that the immersed form of the heeled hull becomes so asymmetrical that much helm-heaving is required to keep the show on the road.

The more traditional vessels do not suffer from this difficulty. Indeed, some pre-war designers, notably Dr. Harrison Butler, specialized in yachts whose sections were of such sophistication that within reasonable limits, the degree of heel had absolutely no effect on their helm balance. Such yachts were a dream to steer at sea, but were, of course, cramped for the party-goer.

## ROLLING

When a yacht is rolling heavily, the effect of her rig and her changing immersed hull form will generate alternating weather and lee helm. The person steering a beamy, flat-floored boat will need to be permanently on the alert as she swings downwind in hard weather, particularly if the yacht is being driven hard. If she is permitted to roll too far, control may be lost quite suddenly. The result of this is usually a comprehensive broach, which, at best, will be highly unpleasant for all hands.

## Steering with the Sails

Even when a boat is stalled or starting from a standstill, she can nearly always be steered. She still has a pivot point, although it may have become rather spongy, and, if she has more than one sail, she has the capacity to apply force both forward and aft of it.

When a boat is lying beam-on to the wind with all her sails "spilling," the natural tendency is for her head to fall away. This can be counteracted by "bringing on" the mainsheet. As the sail begins to draw, the yacht's head will be forced up to weather. If it looks as though she will come up too far before the rudder has established a grip on the water, the situation can be controlled by hauling in the

Steering with sails

Sheet in main, spill jib, and boat tends to luff up.

Harden in jib sheet, spill wind from main, and boat tends to bear away.

wind

jibsheet so that the sail holds the yacht's head down while she gathers way.

A boat can be encouraged to luff by assisting her to heel by hauling in the mainsheet, while the cause of bearing away rapidly is doubly served by letting the same sheet out. Not only will this action get rid of all power abaft the pivot point, it will also tend to bring the yacht more upright and lessen the tendency to luff brought about by heeling.

When she is moving well through the water with her keel and rudder firing on all cylinders, a modern boat will often sail controllably under mainsail or jib alone. Some will even develop weather helm while they are setting nothing but a genoa. This apparent contradiction in terms is explained by the heeling of the boat, but the general point to remember is this: If all other things are equal, any sail drawing abaft the pivot point is encouraging the boat to turn her head to windward, while any sail forward of it is trying to persuade her to bear away.

The ramifications of this simple statement pervade all boat handling under sail, whether you are crossing the Pacific on a fast broad reach, hove to in a Biscay gale, or maneuvering through a crowded anchorage to a suitable berth. Acting upon it can save time and wear-

and-tear when on passage. In harbor, it will make the difference between tidy maneuvers and hit-and-miss, sling-her-in-and-hope-for-the-best attempts. The majority of such ill-informed efforts end up in the "miss" category, while the "hits" show a nasty tendency to make an expensive end to what could otherwise have been a perfect day.

# 2 THEORY OF SAIL-POWER

Back in the 1950s, sailing a sloop was a simple business. All you had to do was choose your sails, pull them up hard, sheet them in until their luffs stopped lifting, and glide away into the sunset. A few minor rig adjustments were becoming available, such as movable jib-sheet fairleads and adjustable mainsail clew outhauls, but essentially there was little that could be done to alter the shape of the sails. They were cut to a form somewhere between what the owner thought he wanted and what the sailmaker was sure he ought to have. That became their shape, and there it stayed until old age or honest abuse blew it out of them. Only then was the owner driven back to the loft for another ten rounds with the palm-and-needle boys.

Time and a developing awareness of the potential of modern materials have changed all that. Even on cruising boats we now have sails whose shape can be adjusted within certain broad limits to suit any conditions in which they are capable of being set. The majority of today's yachts are equipped with the necessary gear to effect these changes, and the net result is that individual sails are more tolerant of varying wind strengths, while today's rigs can turn out far more usable power than their predecessors could.

There is, however, a catch. If we fail to use this wonderful gear to its best advantage, it can actually work against us. A stretch-luff genoa improperly set up in a stiff breeze will be far less effective than its old-fashioned "grind-it-up-tight-and-go-for-broke" equivalent. However, in able hands, the modern sail will lift the boat higher to windward and make her heel far less. It all depends on the user.

Similarly, we've all seen those amazing pictures of yachts racing before the days of the center boom vang. The twist on the mainsails looks unbelievable to our eyes, with what appears to be half the wind being ditched without ceremony from the upper portion of the sails. The young may feel that they are observing a maritime example of artistic license, but older hands will confirm that boats really were sailed that way. Now we have at least two controls for checking the boom's tendency to rise; but do we know how much we should be controlling it? Heave too hard on the vang at the wrong time, and the boat is killed just as efficiently as it was by the absence of a vang altogether. It's up to us to get it right.

Contrary to the blusterings of those who prefer to remain unenlightened, this sort of talk isn't to do with tuning hot-shot racers, it's about giving a cruiser a decent, seamanlike chance to perform properly and award her people a smooth, quiet ride. A yacht with properly trimmed sails not only goes faster (and may thus save her tide, anchor before sunset, tie up before the pubs shut, or whatever else motivates her crew to move her along), she also travels more comfortably.

The art of close-quarters boat handling rests upon an ability to sail along the edge of a stall, but until the operation of a modern rig is fully understood, it cannot be used convincingly to slow the boat down. Unlike the driver of a road vehicle, a sailor needs to be able to go fast before he can properly control a slow-moving boat. So, here goes! We'll start by considering how a sail actually works, and then progress from there.

## Sails

It is obvious to anyone who has ever looked at a setting sail that it is not a flat piece of canvas. It is cunningly cut and stitched so that it has curvature as well as length and breadth. What is not so blatant is how this triangle of cloth propels a boat in any direction other than dead downwind. The basic misconception normally held by the laity is that a sail is a bag to catch the breeze. "The wind puffs into the bag," they fondly imagine, "and the yacht is blown along."

In reality, unless the boat is on a dead run this is never the case. When the sail is set properly, the wind blows smoothly around both sides of the curved cloth. As it does so, the sail generates lift by forming a zone of low pressure on its leeward, or convex side, into which the boat is effectively sucked.

It is easier to understand how this is achieved if, instead of thinking of the air flowing past the sail as the colorless gas that it is, we imagine it as two lines of table-tennis balls flying along in pairs. As they arrive at the luff of the sail, the two lines are separated so that one ball of each pair flies around the convex side, and the other around the concave side. Shortly after they have cleared the leech of the sail, each ball joins up with its opposite number once again and disappears from the picture, having done its job well. All that appears to have happened is that the streams of balls have been parted from one another, and deflected in direction. A further analogy will clarify how this contrives to generate a pressure difference.

Instead of table-tennis balls flying around the sail, imagine two ranks of soldiers marching down a straight road, one rank on either side of the road, and each soldier abeam of his opposite number. The files approach a bend in the road. As they negotiate the turn, the soldiers on the outside lengthen their stride and accelerate in order to maintain station opposite their buddies, while the soldiers on the inside shorten their stride and slow down.

Now, go back to the table-tennis balls. As they fly around the curved sail, the ones on the leeward, or outside of the sail accelerate just as the soldiers did, and the ones on the inside slow down or, if they are cutting the corner, maintain pace. As the outside balls speed up, they spread out one from another. There are fewer of them to the square foot of sail now, so they exert less pressure than their colleagues on the other side. Substitute the idea of the little white balls with the concept of molecules of air dashing about, and you have the answer: A pressure difference is established across the sail.

## The Slot Effect

Where two sails are used in conjunction with one another, the power of the system is increased by something greater than the extra area which is available. The air that is flowing across the inside of a head-sail is the same as that which is about to be accelerated around the back of the mainsail. This airstream is being squeezed through the gap, or slot, between the two sails. Any flowing gas that is compressed in this way is accelerated by the *venturi effect,* so the air that is creating lift as it comes around the back of the headsail will also have to speed up, pro rata, in order to keep pace with events. The whole rushing mass then rips around the lee side of the mainsail, whose effect is pepped up dramatically. If the headsail happens to be a genoa, the overlap between it and the forward portion of the main-sail substantially "deepens" the slot, which powers up the effect still further.

In practice, seamen have known about this for generations, but just to make sure it wasn't a myth, a series of experiments were performed some years ago by a reputable scientific organization. A strain gauge was connected to a genoa sheet in a wind tunnel, and the force on the sheet was noted. When a mainsail was set up in the correct place abaft the genoa, the strain on the headsail sheet was observed to rise considerably. After that, there was no room for argument.

## Sail-Power and Forward Progress

The lifting force generated by a sail is in a direction approximately at right angles to a line joining luff and leech. On the face of things, this suggests that a closehauled yacht should be blown almost side-ways. The reason why this does not happen is that she has no wish to go that way on account of her keel and her general inherent resist-ance to sideways forces. On the contrary, her one desire is to oblige by going ahead, if this is at all possible.

The force of the closehauled sail is best understood by resolving it theoretically into two smaller forces: a forward component and a sideways component. If these two forces could be synthesized and persuaded to act simultaneously, they would produce an identical effect to the actual force of the sail itself. The diagram shows that when the yacht's sails are sheeted close to her mid-line, the forward component is considerably less than its sideways partner. However, such is the lateral resistance of a well-designed sailing vessel that she is able to soak up nearly all the sideways force, leaving the diminutive forward component to work its magic against the yacht's equally small resistance to forward movement. The result, against all the apparent odds, is forward progress.

Unfortunately, the whole of the sideways component of the force of the rig can never be gobbled up by the yacht's keel. Broadly speaking, the residual is manifested as leeway and the heeling of the vessel. The more efficient the keel and the rig, the less are the heeling and leeway, and the more effective is the push in the right direction.

As the wind moves aft and sails are sheeted farther from the centerline of the boat, the forward component of the sails increases while the sideways force diminishes. Once the apparent wind (see Chapter 7) is established just abaft the beam, the sails can drive with maxi-

The forward drive of a close-hauled sail

wind

Forward driving force

Resultant force

Sideways force

When a sail is closehauled, the forward component of its resultant force is so small that every effort must be made to maximise its effectiveness.

The forward drive of a sail on a beam reach

wind

Forward driving force

Resultant

Sideways force

A sail set correctly to a beam wind creates a powerful forward component to drive the boat ahead.

mum efficiency until the wind comes so far aft that they can no longer be sheeted to allow the air to flow around them properly. At this point, they become no more than the wind-bags of the layman's fancy, and the boat slows down onto a dead run.

This is all very well, but it only works so long as the air is flowing cleanly around the sail. Once the airstream detaches itself on one side or the other, the "pairs of soldiers" will no longer remain opposite one another, the "table-tennis balls" will not rejoin their opposite numbers at the leech of the sail, and the whole lift-generating mechanism will begin to break down.

## CORRECT SAIL TRIM/SHEETING

The trim of a sail is the angle at which it is being presented to the wind. This depends upon the helmsman when the boat is closehauled and the sails are hauled right in; when she is reaching or running, the sheets are adjusted until the correct setting has been achieved. Trimming a sail and shaping it are best thought of as two different things, but sail shape will be considered later.

There are three main states of sail trim:

**Undersheeted.** In this condition, either the sheet has been eased too far, or, if the boat is closehauled, she is being steered too close to the wind (see Chapter 5). The effect is that the luff of the sail "lifts" and the airflow breaks down, particularly on the windward side.

**Correctly sheeted.** Here, everything is working fine; the sail is being presented to the wind at the correct angle, and is pulling as well as it is able.

**Over-sheeted.** When the sail is sheeted too close to the boat's centerline, or when a closehauled boat is steered below (to leeward of) her best course to windward, the sail is said to *stall*. It may look deceptively well set, but air is breaking away from its leeward side. In this condition the sail is producing minimal lift and an overdose of the dreaded leeway and heeling.

Constant vigilance is required aboard any yacht to ensure that her sails are correctly sheeted. Aboard a racing boat, the matter is receiving continuous attention. Depending upon the circumstances and the character of the individual, a cruising skipper will certainly back off from this ideal, but no sailor worthy of the name will sail for hours with the genoa apparently full without easing the sheet periodically to check for stalling. After a while, this process becomes second nature and a matter of personal pride. The very thought of great chunks of air whirling around all over the place only a few feet off the deck when the whole wind engine should be in a state of harmonious flow ought to spoil any seaman's day.

## Camber

We have discussed how the lift of a sail derives from the fact that it offers a curved surface to the airstream. The deeper the curvature, or *camber,* the more the airflow will be bent and, so long as the air does not detach from the sail, the greater will be the power of the system.

The most notable difference between the sails of today and their antecedents is that we now have the ability to control the state of their curvature. In light airs a deep camber may be required, while with increasing wind strengths it will be desirable to flatten the same sail progressively so that it will not overpower the boat. All this is possible with modern gear.

It is critical that the point of maximum camber is maintained in

Camber

Correct camber-
maximum curve
about 40% aft
from luff.

Incorrect
camber-
Curvature abaft the
mid-point of the
sail is counter productive.

the correct fore-and-aft position. For a genoa, this is generally about 40 to 45 percent of the distance from luff to leech. A mainsail set abaft a headsail may prefer its camber at 50 percent, but no sail, under any circumstances, should be carried when its camber moves irreversibly farther aft than that. At this point, the sail will be so inefficient as to be a gross embarrassment to the yacht's performance.

The way camber is adjusted in practice will be studied in the next chapter, but you should never lose sight of the fact that unless the helmsman is sailing the yacht steadily on her course, any attempt to set up the rig is going to be a waste of time.

# 3 LETTING HER GO: SHAPING THE SAILS

"Oh Lord, let her go!" was the anguished cry aboard many a nineteenth-century sailing ship as the shellbacks groaned to see their charge being poorly sailed by the skipper. Paradoxically, the same phrase was uttered in joy from time to time as the Old Man got it right in a strong breeze and a thousand tons of clipper thundered away at 15 knots, but it must be said that even in those halcyon days, sails were often set less well than they might have been. No doubt as a ship slugged along at 7 knots when 10 should have been the mark, the sea-lawyers would smirk and say, "More days, more dollars," but that would do little to cheer the spirits of the real sailors. A vessel doing less well than she could have been was anathema to them, just as this ought to be to us.

This does not necessarily mean that we should all turn into Black Ball Line skippers and risk the safety of our yachts by desperate driving. What we want is to see our boats sailed in such a way that they can deliver us to our destination in as short a time and in as great a degree of comfort as they are reasonably able.

We have dealt with the essential theory of the matter in the previous two chapters. In this one we'll examine how to deal with the sails in practice so that a yacht can do herself justice.

The basic proposition of how a sail should be *trimmed* is understood by every yachtsman, but as we have seen, before a modern sail can be trimmed effectively it must be the right *shape* for the day on which it is set. The two concepts are entirely separate and must be treated as such. Attempting to sheet a sail that has not been set up properly for the current conditions is like trying to write on the waves.

## Control of Camber

### HEADSAILS

The only effective control of camber in a cruising yacht headsail is halyard tension. As the halyard winch is wound on harder, the camber of the sail moves forward; as it is eased off, the camber moves aft. How dramatic this movement is depends on the sail, but all soft-luffed sails are affected to a certain extent.

Camber is best checked by looking up at the middle part of the sail. If the sail has a "go-faster stripe" (a dark, horizontal stripe, running from luff to leach, that makes the camber—or lack of it—clearly visible), the job is easy. If there is no stripe, the curvature of the sail can be judged well enough by reference to the seams.

The sail should be hoisted, then sheeted in a closehauled state before deciding how much tension to apply. If the breeze is light, the halyard should be wound up *gently,* watching the sail all the time. When the camber is about 45 percent aft of the luff, that will do.

When the wind strength increases, the camber will be "blown" aft as the sail stretches. Once this begins to happen, the halyard should be cranked up harder until sail shape is restored. At even higher wind speeds, the tension is further increased; at this stage it may be found necessary to move the sheet fairlead aft (see the following section) so that the camber remains where it should be as the sail is flattened right off.

As soon as the wind has risen to a degree where no amount of tweaking can maintain the sail in the shape it should be, the time has come to change down to a smaller, flatter-cut sail, or to take a few rolls if the sail on the stay is a roller-reefer. If the sail has been expertly made and the sail wardrobe is well planned, this moment will coincide with the point at which the boat can no longer carry that area of sail, no matter how well cut it may be.

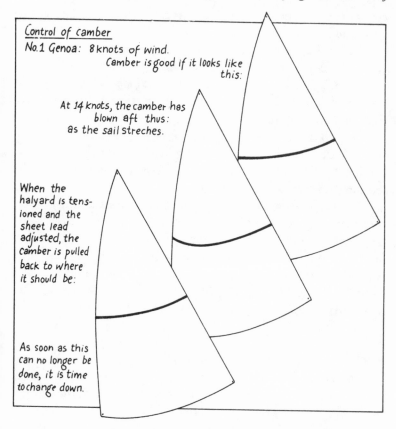

Control of camber
No.1 Genoa: 8 knots of wind.
Camber is good if it looks like this:

At 14 knots, the camber has blown aft thus: as the sail streches.

When the halyard is tensioned and the sheet lead adjusted, the camber is pulled back to where it should be:

As soon as this can no longer be done, it is time to change down.

## MAINSAILS

Mainsail camber is controlled by luff tension in just the same way as that of a headsail, but because the main is set on a boom, it usually enjoys the additional facility of a clew outhaul. The two are used in conjunction to achieve the desired result, remembering that the camber of the main is often best when it is only fractionally forward of the middle of the sail. One of the reasons for this is that if the camber is too far forward, the sail will have what is called a "hard entry," which may cause it to be backwinded by the air coming through the slot. This is more noticeable when a boat is masthead rigged. The fractional-rig mainsail is often cut to carry its camber farther forward, to the 40-percent mark.

The way to find the best result is to experiment and *look at your results*. The camber must never be abaft the center of the sail and, ideally, no part of the sail should be backwinded when the boat is closehauled. This latter proposition may sometimes be compromised, but NEVER the former.

Some boats have no easy method of adjusting the clew outhaul, but it is usually possible on smaller boats to heave the clew in and out by hand. If this is not convenient, a healthy compromise will be required on the question of foot tension.

Practically speaking, it is worth remembering that the gear on most cruising yachts will not be powerful enough to effect major adjustments to the shape of a sail that is full of wind. In particular, attempts to tackle the tension of clew outhauls and halyards, or to shift sheet-lead positions with the sails drawing, are more likely to lead to internal injuries of your crew than to a flatter sail. The answer is, of course, to momentarily relieve the load by easing the sheet.

**A Cunningham hole** is to be found a foot or so above the mainsail tack on some cruiser/racers. A line passed through this can be hauled down in order to increase luff tension without touching the halyard winch. A "Cunningham" is important if a boat is racing, because it allows the luff of the main to be tensioned when to wind up the halyard any further would mean raising the head of the sail above the measured mark on the mast, with a resulting risk of penalty. Alternatively, if the sail is cut to achieve "full hoist" in moderate airs, the only way of bringing on the tension in a harder breeze will be to heave down on the Cunningham.

On some sail and mast setups, luff groove or slide friction will mean that increasing halyard tension tends to affect the upper part of the sail more than the lower, particularly if the job can be done with wind in the sail. An adjustment of the Cunningham produces an immediate and dramatic result in the bottom third of the sail.

**Flattening reefs** are often built into high-performance cruising sails. A "flattener" has only one cringle, which is to be found in the leech of the sail. It is used on occasions when the sail is too full for the prevailing conditions, but not yet so oversized that a reef is needed.* The flattener works by taking out the fullness from the foot of the sail.

**Leech lines** are to be found in the majority of today's cruising sails. Put bluntly, these pieces of string are, for most of us, a necessary evil. The leech line in either a jib or a mainsail is there to ensure that the leech does not flutter, and is not "hooked" either. The way to let it best achieve this for a given sail shape is to slack it away until the leech begins to beat, then bring it on again just sufficiently to put the sail to sleep, and no further.

Note that many mainsails now have neat little jam cleats for the leech line immediately above each reef cringle. This is so that adjustments can be made to the reefed sail. They are generally arranged in such a way that after the reef has been shaken out, any tweaking from the position of "the next cleat down" will release the line from the one above it.

On some sails, leech lines are big on nuisance value, requiring considerable attention, but without them our nights would be sleepless as our leeches beat themselves noisily to expensive destruction.

## TWIST

You'll have noticed that most boats seem to exhibit a certain amount of *twist* between the angle of attack of the bottom and top of their sails. This is not a matter of chance. It does not occur because it is impossible to control a sail well enough to keep it from happening (it used to, but it doesn't anymore); rather, it is an important consideration in the search for boat speed and should be watched carefully.

---

*Reefing in order to reduce sail area will be covered in Chapter 4.

A sail needs to twist because the apparent wind (see Chapter 7) which it is bending is blowing at different speeds 10 feet and 30 feet above the water. Surface friction between the flowing air and the sea's face is slowing down the breeze at deck level more than it is at the masthead. The slower the airstream, the more the speed of the boat modifies it in strength and direction. Since the boat's movement is tending to pull the wind angle forward, the lower part of the sail will need to be sheeted closer to the boat's centerline than the upper part if the whole sail is to set sweetly. The amount of twist required for a given sail will depend on the wind speed, so sails require adjustment to take it into account.

## Twist

Because the wind speed is higher aloft than at deck-level, the wind in the upper portion of a sail is less affected by the boat's progress than that at the foot. The lower part of the sail must therefore be sheeted closer to the boat's centre line than the upper portion in order that the whole sail should draw sweetly.

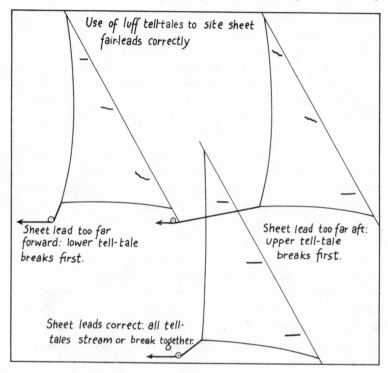

Use of luff telltales to site sheet fair-leads correctly

Sheet lead too far forward: lower tell-tale breaks first.

Sheet lead too far aft: upper tell-tale breaks first.

Sheet leads correct: all tell-tales stream or break together.

## HEADSAILS

The twist of a headsail (and to a certain extent the camber, as noted above) is controlled by the fore-and-aft position of the sheet fairlead. The primary sources of visual information on the subject are luff telltales. Every boat should have three or four of these lengths of wool evenly spaced up the luffs of her jibs, 5 or 6 inches abaft the luff tape, or rope. If your sails do not have them, they can be installed in minutes with a palm and needle. Eight-inch lengths of one-ply darning wool are punched through the sail, and knotted on either side of the cloth.

All that is required to set the fairlead correctly is to sheet the sail closehauled, steer on the wind, and look at the telltales. You'll have started out with the fairlead placed so that the imaginary line drawn onward from the sheet into the sail meets the luff about 40 percent of the way from tack to head. If all is well, the telltales will be streaming cleanly aft on both sides of the sail. Note what happens if the boat is pointed too "high"; the windward, or inside telltales will lift and begin to flutter well before the luff of the sail crumples. If the boat is stalled by steering too far off the wind, the telltales on the lee side will collapse, indicating that air has broken away from outside the sail (see Chapter 1). If the twist of the sail is incorrect, its angle of attack will vary with height up the luff. The result is demonstrated by the fact that one windward telltale will break before the others as the boat is brought steadily toward the wind.

When the bottom telltale goes first, it shows that the lower portion of the sail is too full. This can be cured by moving the fairlead farther aft so as to flatten the foot of the sail and "open" the leech. On the other hand, if the lead is too far aft, the sheet will be pulling the foot of the sail into a board-like shape, while the upper sections will be twisting off, lacking the necessary leech tension to form them properly. This state is indicated by the upper windward telltales lifting before the others. It is cured, needless to say, by sliding the fairlead forward a few notches.

Once the sheets are eased and the boat is reaching, the telltales are used to achieve the optimum *set,* but remember that as the boat bears away, the apparent wind speed may alter sufficiently to render the luff tension too great. This will spoil the shape of the sail. It only takes a second or two to ease the halyard, and if this wins you ¼ knot of boat speed, remember that this is worth 1 hour in 24 at 6 knots!

Further control over the flow of air across a headsail can be achieved by using a *barber-hauler.* Sometimes, try as you will, you cannot set up the shape you want without, for example, backwinding the mainsail. This can be particularly annoying on a close reach. A way to cure the situation is to rig a line from the clew of the sail outboard to a block on the toerail, thence to a spare winch in the cockpit. The sheet is eased an inch or two and this new line, or barber-hauler, is brought into play to heave the clew of the sail farther from the boat's mid-line. The effect is to "open the slot" without compromising the shape of the genoa. Most cruisers do not enjoy the facilities for such refinements of sail shape, but where they exist, they can be genuinely effective over a long leg of a passage.

## MAINSAILS

Luff telltales don't work at all well on mainsails, because the presence of the mast interferes with the airflow over that portion of the sail. However, it is useful to know how cleanly air is running off the leech. If the leech is hooked to windward, for example, eddies will form around it which will slam on the air brakes with deadly efficiency. Some sails arrive from the sailmaker's with leech telltales built in. If yours does not, a few 4-inch lengths of light fabric tape sewn into the outboard ends of the batten pockets will serve perfectly. Twist in mainsails is easily controlled, readily spotted, and affects not only boat speed, but also helm balance. Too little twist at the wrong time will pile up weather helm mercilessly as well as slowing you down. A modicum of attention paid to this department of the wind engine will repay your trouble many times over.

Mainsail twist can be judged roughly by a quick check of how the curve of the leech is following that of the headsail. A finer gauge is found by looking up the after part of the sail from beneath the boom. If the top batten is running parallel to the boom itself, you have a good compromise. At that point the leech telltales will probably all be flying free. If they are not, and generally it is the upper ones that misbehave, then it is time to attend to the twist of the sail.

The most important all-around controls of mainsail twist are the center boom vang and the mainsheet. Both regulate leech tension. The sheet also adjusts the *trim* of the sail (how far it is set from the centerline of the boat) for much of the time, but when the yacht is closehauled or close reaching, this is taken care of by the *traveler*, leaving the sheet free to shape the leech.

This combined use of sheet and traveler to shape up and then trim the mainsail is one of the most misunderstood subjects in yachting.

When the sail is closehauled, the sheet is pulling more or less down on the leech. If the boom vang is let off, the sheet itself will check the amount the boom end rises, and so control twist.

Once the desired shape has been obtained with sheet, halyard, and outhaul, the sail's angle of attack is set by sliding the sheet blocks along the traveler. In light airs, with a big genoa set, you may find that in order to stop the mainsail luff from lifting while keeping the telltales flying, the boom needs to be placed on, or almost on, the centerline of the boat. This is perfectly acceptable. What will not do is for the boom itself to move to windward of the centerline. This demand does not, however, apply to the position of the lower sheet block on the traveler. Often, in very light going, the desired twist can only be found by pulling the block well to windward of amidships and easing the sheet so that the boom rises onto the mid-line.

As the breeze hardens, the sail will twist more just when you probably want it to twist less. When this happens, you heave down on the sheet, usually hardening the halyard to firm up the camber at

Shaping a close-hauled mainsail using the traveller

Traveller used to achieve maximum leech tension and minimum twist: sail flat

Traveller in the amid-ships position so as to allow boom end to lift and encourage the sail to twist:

leech 'open', sail full

Centre boom-vang

Once the boat is squared away with the boom end well outboard the sheet can no longer control the twist of the sail.

Now the vang takes over. In a cruiser it is usually less efficient than the sheet-and-traveller combination, but it is more than adequate for off-the-wind requirements.

the same time. The sail will now be considerably flatter, and you will probably find that the sheet block can be dropped down the traveler to leeward. This will have the double benefit of providing more forward drive (see Chapter 2) and also easing the helmsman's pain by reducing the boat's tendency to heel and round up to windward.

In windy weather, when a small headsail is set and the main is well reefed, it may even pay to let the sheet block run right down to the bottom of the traveler while going to windward.

On a racing yacht, the center boom vang may be in use when closehauled to help flatten the bunt of the mainsail, but on a cruising yacht this is rarely necessary. This particular control comes into its own when trim considerations on a reach or run have called for the mainsheet to be eased "beyond the end of the traveler." Because of its shorter lever arm, the vang will not control the leech of the sail as successfully as did the sheet, but by this time the forward component of the rig has increased sufficiently for the whole business of sail shape and trim to be somewhat less critical.

Finally, a word of warning: The top leech telltale on a high-aspect-ratio (tall and narrow) mainsail can be a demon to put to sleep. Don't forget that you're out there for fun, and the thing will spoil your day if you let it. It's only there as a guide. So long as that upper batten is in the right sort of alignment, you won't go far wrong.

Don't forget, the traveler is there to *trim* the sail when you are closehauled or close reaching. On these points of sailing, the task of the mainsheet is to *shape* it.

Set up with these guidelines in the skipper's mind, a boat will always give of her best on passage. She will go fast, she will be easy on her helmsmen, and she will heel far less, all of which combine to encourage the great cruising virtues: comfort, speed, and low-stress yachting.

# *4* SHORTENING SAIL

In the last chapter, we discussed how to help a yacht to move as well as she can under full sail, but there comes a time, however well the rig is set up, when every boat is overpressed by this amount of canvas. That is the time to shorten down.

## Signs That a Boat Is Overpressed

### EXCESSIVE ANGLE OF HEEL

This is the most obvious pointer to the fact that it is time to reduce canvas. When the toerail disappears under the water, most boats are not only becoming extremely uncomfortable, they are also sailing less efficiently. The further the boat heels, the more her keel is struggling to grip the water, and the more leeway she will make.

Sea state has a considerable effect on how far a boat can be allowed to heel. In calm water, she can drag her rail through the gusts, if she is in a hurry; whereas in a heavy sea, a wind of similar character will have her falling off every wave and burying her decks to the hatches. Not only is this stressful for her victims, it also threatens to shake the yacht and her rig to pieces.

### POTENTIAL RIG DAMAGE

Gear failure is less of a problem with present-day equipment than it was in times gone by. The sails and rigging on a well-found yacht

35

will stand even if she is blown down onto her beam ends. This was not always so; sailors in pre-war, pre-polyester and pre-stainless-steel yachts had always to consider the possibility that if they drove a boat too hard, they might tear the stick clean out of her. Nonetheless, even a Dacron sail will suffer in the long term by being habitually set in more wind than it was designed to bear. The shape will be blown out of it by the constant excessive stretching to which it has been subjected.

While the wind alone may do little immediate damage to a yacht, the lurch of an overpressed vessel crashing hard off a steep wave may provide a snatching force that is enough to break something. It does not do to become overconfident of one's gear.

### EXCESSIVE WEATHER HELM

Helm angle increases with heel, and excess weather helm is usually the most unambiguous indication that it is time to reef or change down. On the beamy, flat-floored boats favored by many designers of production cruisers, weather helm often increases drastically as the boat leans away from the wind. In some cases, it can suddenly become so extreme that the yacht takes charge and flies up into the wind, despite the best efforts of a good helmsman to control her. Long before this stage is reached, the helm will be telling the experienced skipper that it's high time something was done to ease the boat.

## Tactical Sail Reduction

The available options for reducing sail on any Bermudian-rigged yacht are to reduce headsail area by either rolling in a reef or changing down, to reef the mainsail, or to reef or drop the mizzen if there is one. What you decide to do will depend on the boat and the circumstances. If you are carrying a large, full-cut headsail, for instance, it usually pays to exchange it for a flatter, smaller alternative as your first move. If your boat is equipped with a well-cut furling genoa, a few rolls in that is by far the easiest initial reduction. However, if the headsail is not overpowering the boat, it is usually best to put a reef in the mainsail.

Reefing the main serves the cause in two ways: It reduces sail area and lowers the center of effort of the rig, thus diminishing the tendency for the boat to heel. Also, however, by moving the clew inboard along the boom, it shifts the center of effort of the sail forward and closer to the yacht's center of pivot (see Chapter 2). This reduces her desire to luff, and eases the weather helm as a result.

When one is sailing a boat with something other than the rigs described in the preceding paragraphs, the options for sail reduction will be other than those described. The gaff cutter, for example, will first take in her jib topsail, followed by the main topsail. Some ketch-rigged fishing smacks were so short of effective luff length in their mainsails that they preferred to leave the topsail set above a reefed mainsail. Schooners have all sorts of possibilities open to them, and so on.

As long as the principles involved are fully understood, it should be possible for a good skipper to sail a type of craft strange to him, yet still make an intelligent guess as to his first move when the breeze pipes up.

The process of reducing sail can be all joy and ease, or it can be a horror show from which all hands recoil, and which the skipper puts off until matters have become so desperate that Sinbad himself would turn away if invited to go forward to the halyard winch. The choice is in the skipper's hands.

First, the skipper needs to be completely at home with his gear, and second, he must know how to handle his boat so that the job of shortening down can be done without needless drama.

## Reefing the Mainsail

Given that the wind is forward of the beam so that the sail can spill wind, the secret of reefing any mainsail is to have a *routine*. Presented with the correct sequence of actions, any sail will lie down like a lamb; but woe to the sailor who does things in the wrong order. He ends up doing battle with an untamed beast.

## SLAB REEFING

For good reason, this is the most popular system of reefing. It is quick to execute, kind to the sail, and it results in a fine set once the reef is in. This is the sequence:

- Release the vang and sheet to depower the sail.
- Top up the boom with the topping lift. This ensures that the boom doesn't brain the cockpit gang when the halyard is released. It also relieves the weight of the spar from the leech of the sail, which makes hauling down the clew cringle much easier.
- Ease away the halyard, and secure the tack cringle on the reefing hook, or lash it to the boom gooseneck.
- Set up the halyard to ensure that the tack stays on the hook.
- Haul down the clew cringle, using the correct reefing pennant, which should be permanently rove. In small craft this may be done by a straight pull, but in a vessel of any tonnage a winch or a tackle will be required.
- Ease the topping lift, set up the vang, and sheet in.
- The reef can now be tied in using points, if fitted, or a lacing if they are not. On many vessels these days, tying in the reef is a sophistication that is not required except in unusually hard weather, or on occasions when the yacht is "on show." Indeed, the increasingly popular fully battened mainsail self-stows in its lazyjacks, requiring no attention whatever other than to pull down tack and clew. In the case of an old-fashioned boat with a long boom, however, it will be found necessary to tie in the reef every time.

## ROLLER REEFING

The method of reefing by rolling the boom around while easing the main halyard is rarely seen nowadays. Historically, it was used on

Slab reefing: A mnemonic helps maintain an ordered, 4-stage sequence: here is a suggestion:

| Desmond | Depower |
|---------|---------|
| Sought | Support |
| Tamsin's | Tack |
| Consent | Clew |

Depower:
sheet off,
kicker off.

Support:
topping lift set
up to support
boom.

Tack:
ease halyard,
hook on tack
reef cringle, set
up halyard again.

Clew:
reef pennant hauls
clew cringle down
onto boom.

Reef is now complete. All that remains is to tie in the points (if required), ease away topping lift, set up sheet and kicker, and let draw.

gaff-rigged British pilot cutters a century ago and worked very well physically, though the pilots had to accept a trade-off in terms of poor sail shape. From those days through into the 1960s, roller reefing was used on some yachts, but it was never truly satisfactory after the introduction of the Bermudian, or three-cornered mainsail. On these rigs, the sail tended to become fuller as it was reefed more deeply, which is the opposite of what is desirable. Furthermore, the boom end often drooped ever lower, threatening the skull integrity of the cockpit crew. Specially shaped booms, or the addition of tapered battens to their outboard ends, helped considerably, but once modern slab reefing with winches and tack hooks became available, the death knell of roller reefing was sounded, amid sighs of general relief.

For those mariners who are left with roller reefing and can see no realistic possibility of switching to a happier system, the operating technique is logical:

- Unlace the reefing line if one is fitted (this secures the lower part of the luff to the slides in the mast groove).
- Remove the center boom vang from the boom.
- Top up, and roll away.
- As in slab reefing, the sail should ideally be spilling wind as it is reefed.
- Some center boom vangs have a claw arrangement enabling them to be left rigged while the boom and sail are rolled inside them. This arrangement offers a big advantage over any other system, because only in this way can the reefed sail enjoy the benefit of this basic shaping control.

## OTHER METHODS

The introduction of a variety of systems whereby the mainsail is both stowed and reefed by rolling it totally or partially into the mast has revolutionized sail handling. Sad to say, apparent nautical cure-alls generally hide a frowning countenance behind their smiling faces. These reefing arrangements are frequently expensive, the masts that house them are bulky, and failure of the mechanics can cause the proud owner considerable grief and woe.

No doubt, time will ultimately make a good job of in-mast reefing systems; there are signs that it is already doing so. Time will also offer electrical or hydraulic sail handling from the comfort of the skipper's double bunk, at which point that harrassed child of the technological revolution will probably ask himself why he's bothering at all. When the light dawns upon him, I believe that unless he is geriatric, he will rid himself of all such items. They serve, after all, only to insulate him from the reality of his meeting with the elements, and if he craves nothing but ever-greater protection from his chosen environment, he would do well to consider the benefits of motor-yachting.

Put more plainly, it seems a pity to spend all that money on a sail and then never to handle it.

## Smoothing the Way

The handling of a boat while a reef is being taken will make all the difference for the crew. If you get it right, the job will be done quickly so that the foredeck crowd will shamble aft, still dry, and without having had to hang on like rodeo riders on fireworks day.

The answer is to either slow the boat down or stop her altogether. A minimum of time will be lost, because if the hands are properly organized it shouldn't take more than a couple of minutes to reef the mainsail on a 38-foot sloop. A full racing crew worthy of their salt will do the job in 20 seconds.

Think about that.

Just before she is reefed, a 32-footer sailing to windward will be leaping along at 6 knots or so, throwing spray all over the place. Her foredeck will not be an enjoyable place to be, but there are two easy ways of making it more inviting: The first is to take off all way by *heaving to;* the second takes off most of her way by *steering shy.*

### HEAVING TO

When a sloop is hove to, she is stopped in the water by her foresail being sheeted "aback," on the windward side. The mainsail is left drawing to leeward, either closehauled or with an eased sheet, and the whole equilibrium is balanced by the helm, which is lashed so as to try to turn the boat into the wind.

A yacht with a traditional hull form featuring a deep forefoot will maintain herself hove to with the wind well forward of the beam;

indeed, a classic gaff cutter will normally take up what is virtually a closehauled attitude. Unfortunately, the more up-to-date hull forms generally heave to with their bows further off the wind, but by juggling the sheets and tiller they can often be persuaded to improve their act. If the weather jibsheet is eased, the boat heads up; if the main is eased, she will fall off, pushed "down" by the power of the headsail. The boat is balancing around her pivot point (see Chapter 2), and her attitude can be adjusted more or less to suit the needs of the occasion.

Apparently, then, heaving to in order to reef is the ideal answer. Once she is hove to, the boat requires no helmsman, so an extra hand is released to assist at the mast, or to pull down the reef alone if there is no one else on watch. With the traditional hull form, the system worked wonderfully well. Many modern fin-keelers, however, are so delicately balanced about their centers of lateral resistance that when

Heaving-to

This vessel is classically hove to and making no headway. Her backed headsail tries to swivel her head off the wind, while her main and her rudder are attempting to force the opposite effect. The result is an equilibrium which, in some yachts, can be very stable indeed.

Heaving-to by tacking

c. Once the boat has tacked the jib will be aback.
All that is now required to complete the
manoeuvre is to push the tiller to leeward, and experiment
with the sails to discover
the best equilibrium.

a. Sailing close-hauled.

wind

b. Helm is put to leeward
as if to tack, but as the
boat comes through the
wind the jib sheet is NOT
released.

the mainsheet is eased to pull down the reef, the equilibrium is badly
disturbed and the boat falls right off the wind. If a yacht does not do
this, then heaving to is the easiest way for her to encourage the crew
to shorten down in good time, rather than hope the job will go away,
until it is too late.

By far the simplest way to put a yacht into the hove-to state is to
tack her, but, instead of releasing the lee jibsheet as she comes to the
wind, leaving it made fast. As the boat falls onto the new tack, she
will first try to spin on her heel; then, as you push the tiller down to
leeward or wind the wheel to weather, she will make her peace with
the situation and come to a standstill.

If you feel your crew could use the exercise, you can, of course,
winch the jib across to the windward side while the boat is sailing her
course, then move the helm down as she begins to fall off the wind.
She'll heave to, all right, but the winch-men won't like the way
you've done it.

The amount of leeway a boat makes when she is hove to varies
enormously according to her type, but it is important to consider in
the context of this chapter the effect of a genoa. Basically, heaving

to with a genoa set on a masthead rig is a washout. The sail will come aback against the spreaders, where it is immediately at risk of damage. Because of its comparatively large area, it will also overpower the effect of the mainsail, rendering the desired balance almost unobtainable. The effect of a genoa on a fractional rig is less undesirable, but even so, it may prove too much for a satisfactory balance to be achieved.

With either masthead or fractional rigs, creative use of a roller genoa gives you an ideal opportunity to balance the boat when she is hove to.

In a modern yacht, heaving to is usually most useful when the boat is already under short sail, and you are going for the second or third reef. By then, you may well have a working jib set, under which she should heave to without difficulty.

## STEERING SHY

Any boat, at any time, can be restrained in her exuberance by this simple expedient. The sheets are eased and the boat is steered sufficiently above her course to spill wind out of the sails. How much wind you choose to dump will depend on conditions. If there is a

'Steering shy' to slow down boat

Sheets are eased and the boat is steered somewhat 'above' her course. With care, this can reduce speed to the slowest that conditions will allow, so as to make the foredeck a friendlier place.

wind

'Running-off' to change a headsail

c. If sea-room is at a premium, boat is brought back to the wind so as to jog along while foredeck crew do their work.

Jib is dropped.

a. Crashing to windward, over-canvassed. Apparent wind 40 knots.

b. Running off for a few seconds, jib in shelter of mainsail, foredeck dry, apparent wind 28 knots.

wind

lumpy sea running, you'll need a certain amount of way on in order to retain control. If the water is flatter, you'll be able to almost stop, but it is vital that the boat is kept moving just above stalling speed. If she stalls, her head will fall off the wind despite the best efforts of the helmsman, and to allow this to happen when the hands are half-way through a reef is downright insensitive. You'll know when she's about to stall because the wheel or tiller will go "spongy," and she'll suddenly develop lee helm.

## RUNNING OFF FOR HEADSAIL CHANGES

Either of the techniques we have just discussed are also useful when changing a headsail, but you'll have to bear in mind that if you are hove to, the boat will tend to luff as soon as the jib comes down. Nevertheless, heaving to makes that initial journey to the plunging foredeck a great deal less fraught with anguish than would other-wise be the case.

Another way of keeping the acid level down for a headsail change is to run the boat dead downwind for a few seconds while the crew work their way forward to drop the sail. The difference in the con-ditions on the deck of a boat going to windward and one running off is indescribable. Once the sail is on the deck, the yacht can be brought back to the wind again if you are concerned about giving away your weather gauge. Without a headsail set, her way will have fallen off drastically, and so will the violence of her motion.

The only danger attached to this method is that the crew are at risk from the clew of the genoa as it marauds from side to side, unable to decide whether to goose-wing itself or not. The problem can be nullified if you closehaul the monster in the lee of the mainsail. The job won't require any effort on the sheet-winch, and it has the additional benefit of persuading the sail to drop on deck, safely inside the guardrails.

## Combinations of Shortened Sail

The question of which sail combination should be carried when the main is reefed and the number one genoa is back in the locker, is best decided by paying attention to the balance of the helm. The boat should be set up so that when she is sailing close to the wind, she carries just a touch of weather helm. If she is given too much "grunt up front," she may fall off to leeward at every pitch, while if her headsail is too small for the area of mainsail and/or mizzen on display, the helmsman may pass his day with the tiller around the back of his neck.

Your choice of sail will sometimes depend upon whether you are going upwind or downwind. Many a vessel prefers to have a larger proportion of mainsail set while beating in order to help keep her head "up," while broad reaching in a heavy sea may call for more headsail and less main in order to neutralize a tendency to develop weather helm as she rolls.

Like the people that have created them, all boats are different, so let yours talk to you, and give her what she wants. She knows better than you do what that should be, in order to let her go.

# 5 HELMING UNDER SAIL

One of the exercises recommended by the Royal Yachting Association training scheme for dinghy sailors is called "Rudderless Sailing." The student lays his rudder in the bottom of the boat and proceeds to experiment with sail balance and the heeling effects produced by shifting crew weight until sufficient mastery has been achieved to sail the boat upwind, downwind, and on a reach. Before the student is considered competent, he must also tack and jibe without a rudder.

Once you can do this, you can start to call yourself a sailor.

Such maneuvers would be a very different proposition in a cruising yacht because of the impossibility of persuading the boat to heel to windward when required. However, the attitude engendered by the exercise should always remain uppermost in a skipper's mind: The rudder is only a part of the overall system for pointing the boat in the desired direction. If everything else is working in harmony, and the vessel is not being driven hard, a minimum of helm movement should suffice to keep her on the straight and narrow.

A skilled helmsman will be able to reduce even this amount of deflection of the rudder by thoughtful anticipation of the yacht's next move. With practice, this ends up as a deep-seated instinct which corrects the boat's wandering tendencies before they have begun. Such a person will keep a wheel-steered boat reaching in a straight line for the whole of a two-hour trick and never move the helm more than a couple of spokes, which will please the boat mightily. Any excess movement of the rudder slows the yacht down, so it pays to concentrate on learning to feel what she is about. That way you don't fight her, and you satisfy both yourself and her.

## Steering to Windward

In the days of gaff-rigged yachts with long bowsprits and even longer keels, the business of steering to windward was a matter of art and feeling. For much of the time you simply could not see the luff of the jib because it sagged away behind the staysail, so you set the boat in her groove by watching the true wind direction on the water, and by feeling her needs through the seat of your fearnaught trousers. Today, in a well-tuned cruising yacht it is possible to learn in a week what used to take years, because, from the outset, the boat can be sailed accurately to windward by watching the telltales on the jib luff.

Once the rig is set up to the skipper's satisfaction, the responsibility for presenting the whole system of airfoils at the best angle to the flowing air rests with the helmsman. As a general proposition, the telltales on both sides of the jib should be streaming smoothly aft, though in smooth water or strong wind, it may be acceptable to steer so "high" that the *windward* ones flick upward from time to time. The amount that this can be allowed depends on the power available from the rig and on how much the seas are stopping the boat. The feel of the helm and the speed of the boat supply the answer. If she slows too much, her leeway will increase and any apparent gain from the high pointing will be nullified.

A digital speed log is sometimes of great assistance when experimenting to find the best angle to sail a boat toward the wind. Unfortunately, these admirable devices tend to mesmerize the crew so that any gains may be lost as the hands forget what it is they are supposed to be doing. If there is no such instrument on board, the problem does not arise, and the helmsman is back once more to the eyes God gave him and to the seat of his pants. He could do much, much worse.

Often, when the sail combination is just right for the average wind strength, the boat will be struggling in the gusts. When this

Steering to windward
in waves
The technique of luffing to the
crests and bearing away over the
top is well worth practising. If executed to perfection, in a boat that is quick on the helm, it
will reduce pounding to a minimum while producing the best possible speed to windward the circumstances
can allow.

happens, you can luff her gently so that those windward telltales kick up. This will indicate that the rig is ditching some of its power, and you will feel the boat come more upright. So long as you don't overdo it, there will be ample drive left to hammer through the squall, gaining rather than losing ground.

This technique is crucial when sailing a modern boat with a flat 'midship section and a deep fin keel. These yachts cannot be allowed to heel excessively, and constant vigilance is required from the helmsman to "keep them on their feet." If, as sometimes happens despite the "driver's" best efforts, the yacht takes a gust that she cannot handle without screwing up into the wind, he will have to call for the crew to "dump" the traveler until he can regain control. This must be seen as a last-ditch expedient, and if it happens more than once or twice, sail should be shortened accordingly. If this does not help (as is not unknown), then the yacht should be consigned to the scrapheap at the owner's earliest convenience.

At no time when the apparent wind is forward of the beam, but particularly when closehauled, should the *leeward* telltales be allowed to go dancing. The instant they do, the sails are seen to be stalling, which means the boat is being steered too far from the wind. She is not only giving away ground that could have been made good, she is almost certainly heeling far more than she need be. The solution is to luff steadily until the situation is rectified.

## STEERING IN WAVES

When a boat that is quick on the helm (see Chapter 1) is being worked to windward in a seaway, it pays dividends to steer her over the waves in order to prevent her from pounding. The technique is simple to describe, but it takes practice to develop the feel required in order to work it to perfection.

While the boat is approaching the crest of a wave, she is steadily luffed above her proper course. As she traverses the ridge, the helm is brought "up" sharply so that she bears away down the back of the wave rather than falling headlong into the trough and crashing to a teeth-rattling near-standstill. When sailing in regular waves, this technique soon develops into a rhythmic action that seems almost to pump the vessel upwind. In a confused sea the helmsman will need to be on the lookout for any particularly steep waves, and it is to these that he will apply his skill.

Once this process has been mastered and utilized aboard the right sort of yacht, it will make for a measurable improvement over the performance of a similar boat that is sailing in a straight line. The negative results of the extra helm activity and the short periods when the rig is not presented ideally to the airstream are more than compensated for by the way the yacht is negotiating the waves.

Any attempt to work all but the largest waves in a heavy-displacement, long-keeled yacht will be a total waste of time. Fortunately, however, vessels of this type do not make such demands on their helmsmen. They are reluctant to pound in the first place, and even if they do occasionally drop off a steep wave, their displacement and easy sections carry them bravely through. The best way to work such a boat to windward in an awkward sea is to ease the sheets a touch and steer a few degrees off. The additional power created will be more than enough to do the business.

## Steering a Rolling Boat

In the previous chapter we have seen how, as a boat rolls, she is subjected to forces that alternately induce her to round up, then to bear away. Running downwind in hard conditions, either of these can result in a broach, which may have disastrous consequences if the yacht is heavily canvased and being driven hard.

As she rolls to leeward, the necessary weather helm to stop her luffing must be applied; then, as the motion carries the masthead to windward, a helping of lee helm will be required to prevent the dreaded jibe-broach.

A considerable degree of confidence is needed to do this well, especially to hold the tiller down to the lee side of the cockpit as the boat makes to roll over on top of you, but if the job is skillfully done, not only will the yacht sail straighter, she will also roll less. If, on the other hand, she is allowed to indulge herself, the rolling may increase rhythmically until there is nothing you can do to prevent a broach.

The good helmsman does all this by feel. As the stern lifts to ride down a wave, he or she can tell which way the boat will try to roll and go. The corrective measure will be applied before the dive off-course begins, and the rest of the crew will never know how well the job is being handled until they try it themselves. Because it's done by feel, it works just as well in the dark.

As in all questions of coordination, some people are born more able at downwind steering than others, but all are better for having practiced, tiller in hand, listening with all their senses to what the boat is saying.

## Steering Through a Tack

The process of coming about on a fore-and-aft-rigged yacht should be smooth, well-drilled, and executed with a minimum of hard labor.

Steering through a tack

a. Closehauled on starboard tack. Going well.

b. The helm is put 'down' hard to bring the yacht through the wind as quickly as possible.

c. As she carries her way, the boat is then steered 'shy' of close-hauled until the crew have winched the jib sheet in, which should only take a matter of seconds.

d. When the sheet is home, the yacht fills away on the starboard tack.

wind

It is ironic that this is usually the case on a well-run racing boat, where there is any amount of muscle lying around the deck, as well as big winches to whip in the headsail sheet in a trice.

The fact that the cockpit gorillas hardly need to flex their biceps is due mainly to the quality of the helmsman. If he's skilled, the boat will be brought quickly to the wind and quickly through it, so that the sails are kicking for a minimum of time, but once past the wind's eye the boat will be held a trifle high of the new tack for the few seconds it takes to grind in the headsail sheet. As soon as the sheet is home, the boat bears away onto a closehauled heading and fills her sails. If the whole crew gets it right, the 90-degree turn will appear as a clean curve, and no one will have had to haul in a large genoa full of wind.

The converse of this ideal piece of teamwork occurs when the person at the helm is so thrilled to have contrived to steer through the wind that he promptly falls off onto a beam reach, leaving his winch-grinders sweating and cursing. As the ship's head wanders around looking for the closehauled groove, the long-suffering manual workers are left with the task of winding in yards of unwilling sheet which their leader has thoughtlessly donated to their cause.

Think about the folks in front of you when you're helming through stays. If you give them a chance to work properly, the tack will be faster as well as kinder to all concerned.

## Steering Through a Jibe

Over the years, the business of jibing has received more than its share of bad press, for no other reason than that if it is carried out carelessly or by accident in a strong breeze, damage to gear or bodies may result from the untamed anger of the boom.

Accidental jibes are best avoided by rigging a strong preventer anytime it seems necessary. The way to jibe successfully is as follows:

- Steer almost dead downwind, taking care to keep the boat moving straight.
- Sheet the mainsail hard in amidships and *make fast,* at least with a round turn if there is no jamming cleat in the system. In a tiller-steered boat up to about 35 feet long, the helmsman can do this himself, steering with his knees while he hauls in the sheet.
- Steer carefully through the jibe, making sure that the boat turns just far enough for the mainsail to flop across *and no further.* In a hard breeze, the yacht will tend to luff hard as the boom comes over, so you'll have to be ready for it by giving the helm a firm, preventative pull.
- As soon as the situation is well in hand (a matter of only a couple of seconds), the sheet is surged out and the new course taken up.

Steering through a jibe

wind

1. *Steer dead downwind.*

2. *Sheet main in amidships and make fast.*

3. *Steer through jibe, and be ready with opposite helm to check tendency to luff.*

4. *Ease sheet away as soon as possible and set new course.*

- If the boat is of extreme design, it may be necessary to let the mainsheet run as soon as the boom has come across, in order to control the boat's tendency to round up.
- On any yacht which has a mainsheet traveler operated by lines, both ends must be made fast before jibing. The potential for traveler cars to gobble fingers is terrible, and is ignored at your peril.

## Use of Sheets to Assist Course Alterations

### BEARING AWAY

To the informed observer, the greatest enlightenment offered about whether or not someone can sail a boat is what he does as he bears away. Either the mainsheet is instinctively eased as the helm goes up, or it isn't. The mediocre boat handler will heave the tiller to windward, forcing the boat against her will to turn off the wind. Once her new course is established, he will trim the sails. The good skipper, on the other hand, eases the main as the helm comes up; the boat ceases to heel, and all drive is removed from abaft her center of lateral resistance so that she does not try to resist the turn. How can anyone be so brutish as to ask a yacht to fight all the laws that govern her actions? It beats me.

When she's moving slowly, these effects are even more pronounced because the rudder is working poorly, if at all.

At any time, but particularly when the boat is stalled, she can be persuaded to bear away more positively by sheeting in the jib and ditching the mainsheet.

### LUFFING UP

When a boat is moving well, there is rarely a problem persuading her to luff closer to the wind. If the helm is released, she'll find her own way there, given time. However, as she comes up, it is important to keep sheeting in the main, so that there is a continuing source of drive from abaft the center of lateral resistance.

When a boat is being tacked from a reach to a reach, rather than closehauled, this is even more important. If there is a strong wind and a steep sea, a boat whose mainsheet is ignored may refuse to tack at all.

If the boat is almost, or completely stationary, she can only be made to head up by letting the jib right off and hauling in the mainsheet.

## BACKING THE HEADSAIL

Sometimes a yacht experiences problems in forcing her head through the wind. This should never happen to a well-designed boat that is being sailed properly unless conditions are unusually bad, but if it does, you can always persuade her to complete the maneuver by holding the jibsheet instead of releasing it as the sail begins to lift, then flog. Once the boat is head-to-wind, the sail will fill in the aback position and the ship's head will be pushed across rapidly. As soon as

Tacking with a backed headsail

1. Closehauled on port tack in a heavy sea.

2. Jib sheet is held on as boat comes to the wind. When the sail comes aback, the boat's head is forced rapidly through the wind.

3. As soon as the yacht is established on the starboard tack, the jib sheet is let fly and the jib is sheeted home.

wind

you're sure she's through, release the sheet and haul it in on the "new" side.

This technique is often useful in tight corners, but you should always remember that it may take off the last of the boat's way. When this happens, it becomes necessary to reverse the helm, because the boat will soon be moving astern. Watch her carefully when you back the jib. If you get it wrong, you may cover considerable ground astern before the boat decides to turn onto one tack or the other.

# 6 SLOWING DOWN

In this chapter we'll concentrate on the delicate art of taking way off a boat and sailing her slowly. We've looked at the basic theory of how a boat works, and we've considered some of the skills that are used to help her to go fast. There is now enough information on board to begin looking at the real business of boat handling. Later on in the book we'll sort out the most common day-to-day maneuvers, but for the moment we'll deal with the various available methods of ditching power from the rig without having the yacht blow around like a leaf in the wind.

So long as all her sails can spill wind upon request, there will never be any difficulty experienced in slowing a boat down. The nature of most headsails is such that they can be allowed to flog off their power on virtually any point of sailing. Boomed sails, such as most mainsails, however, are in a different category altogether. It is generally impossible to spill the breeze out of such a sail if the wind is abaft the beam, and it is the ramifications of this basic fact that cause nearly all the problems that are experienced when handling under sail in close quarters. Trying to stop a sailing vessel that has one or more sails drawing is like putting on the brakes of a truck that is running away downhill at full throttle.

## THE CLOSE REACH

On occasions when you are able to plan your strategy to allow the boat to approach an objective on a close reach, you have the ideal circumstance for controlling your speed. If she is sailing at about 60 degrees from the true wind, she can be progressively slowed down by easing the sheets to spill wind. Even if you have misjudged matters so that you need to bear away a few degrees, it will not make much difference because it is possible to spill wind from most mainsails on any heading of up to 75 degrees from the wind's eye. On the other hand, if your situation requires you to haul up a little to windward, you have still 15 degrees to go from your 60 degrees before the boat is closehauled. By then, the forward component of her sail-power will be so weak that if some of it is given away by wind-spilling, the boat will rapidly stall and make leeway into the windward sector. Nothing but a tack or two will extricate her from there, but to avoid it you need only to keep the wind at least 50 degrees on the bow, and all will be well.

If the yacht's speed falls so low while close reaching that she begins to stall, you'll know straight away, because she'll develop lee helm. To correct her, you haul in the mainsheet; as the sail begins to bite, the extra area drawing abaft the pivot point will neutralize the helm and the boat will move gently ahead again. When there is a sea running and more drive is required to retain the keel's grip on the water, this can be achieved by letting draw a part of the jib as well.

wind

The close reach
By spilling a measured amount of wind, speed on a close reach can be controlled to a nicety.

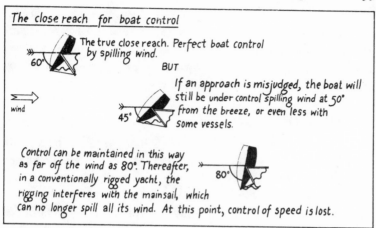

The close reach for boat control

The true close reach. Perfect boat control by spilling wind.

BUT

If an approach is misjudged, the boat will still be under control spilling wind at 50° from the breeze, or even less with some vessels.

wind

Control can be maintained in this way as far off the wind as 80°. Thereafter, in a conventionally rigged yacht, the rigging interferes with the mainsail, which can no longer spill all its wind. At this point, control of speed is lost.

Bring both main and jib sheets on until the leeches of the sails are filling sufficiently to keep the boat moving sweetly.

You cannot beat a close reach for control, but unfortunately, life is such that a boat must frequently be asked to lose way in circumstances that do not allow her that luxury. Suppose you are entering a crowded anchorage downwind on a blustery day. The last thing you want is to come blazing in at 7½ knots, jibing through the boats like a demoniac skier attempting the giant slalom with a head full of drink. In a tideway, you are often prevented by the stream from approaching your mooring or an alongside berth with the wind forward of the beam. There may also be times as you sail up a peaceful river when you might want to dawdle for no better reason than to enjoy the view.

On all these and many other occasions, the question of taking off way *downwind* will arise.

As we have seen, the overriding consideration on a conventionally rigged yacht is that as soon as the wind moves abaft the beam, the mainsail can no longer spill wind because it is pressed against the shrouds; control of speed is therefore lost. The obvious solution is to drop the main and proceed under headsail alone, since headsails can be "feathered" at any wind angle. Sometimes, however, it is useful to be able to leave the main hoisted, but to reduce its drive. For example, it may be required shortly in order to execute a different maneuver; or you may wish to slow down for a few moments in a harbor in order to give way to a commercial vessel.

## STALLING THE MAIN

This provides a reasonable method of spoiling the sail's efficiency. If the wind is on the quarter and you sheet it hard in, it will no longer function as an airfoil. It will still shove the boat along by virtue of its area alone, but its power will be much diminished.

With the wind right aft, a main sheeted onto the centerline of the boat actually feathers from leech to luff as the airflow across it is reversed. Dealt with like this, the sail creates very little push, yet is still there if you need it a few minutes later.

## SCANDALIZING

*Scandalizing* is an even more effective means of achieving the desired result. The center boom vang is disconnected from the boom, the mainsheet is overhauled to its stopper knot, and the boom end is hoisted as high as it can go by hauling away on the topping lift. If your boat has a long enough mainsheet, the effect of all this is most gratifying. The sail flops around not knowing quite what to do, until the lift is released and the power is called up again by pulling in the sheet.

The art of scandalizing was even more effective in the days of gaff mainsails. The boom of the sail was topped a foot or two and the peak halyards (to the outboard end of the gaff) were eased away, instantly reducing sail area by half. If a complete result was looked for, a loose-footed sail could then be made to disappear utterly by tricing the tack up almost as far as the gaff jaws.

If the boat is moving slowly off the wind and she has genuinely finished with her mainsail, the best thing is to drop it, stow it, and forget

Scandalizing the mainsail

topping lift

Most of the power can be dumped from a Bermudan mainsail by overhauling the mainsheet, disconnecting the centre boom-vang and topping the boom up as far as it will go.

The method has the advantage that should power be required again, you have only to let go the topping lift and sheet in.

it. The maneuver can then be completed under headsail alone, controlling speed by spilling wind, as usual.

The biggest problem you are likely to encounter now is that in a strongish breeze, the windage of a flogging genoa may provide sufficient push to keep the yacht trundling along at 2 or 3 knots. This may be faster than you want to go if you are hoping to pick up a mooring or come alongside. The only answer to this is to drop the headsail as well and "blow" along under bare poles. If you are still carrying too much way for your taste, there is not a lot more that you can do about it, short of throwing a bucket over the stern. If your speed should fall too low, you can hoist a few feet of genoa and hold the leech out by hand to catch as much or as little wind as you want.

The boat with a roller headsail, of course, has no such problems.

Perfect downwind speed control is available at a heave of the furling line: no flogging sails; no scrambling around over slippery heaps of canvas on the foredeck to do the human jibsheet act; in fact, nothing to laugh at at all. The roller-furling genoa may leave something to be desired in terms of set when deeply reefed, but as a boat-handling tool it is without peer.

## . . . And Stopping

Just like a motor vehicle that is thrown out of gear, a sailing boat luffed head-to-wind will keep on moving under the impetus of her own momentum until this is exhausted. However, unlike a road vehicle, or to a lesser extent, a vessel under power, the sailing boat has no brakes. She will carry her way until the wind resistance of her flogging sails and her topsides, coupled with her skin friction dragging through the water, combine to snuff it out.

It is vital to understand how far your boat carries her way under varying circumstances. Without this knowledge, all maneuvers under sail are doomed to failure or to the vagaries of pure chance. It is lack of confidence in this matter that, more than any other subject, causes people to fight shy of *sailing* their boats.

The working boatman in the days of sail planned all his movements in harbor with this in his mind. His whole way of thinking revolved around it. He probably even luffed up to his garden gate as he walked home for his tea. The significant difference between him and us is that he never in his life drove a wheeled vehicle with brakes. Because of this, the boat-handling section of his mind was not polluted in the way that ours are.

Whether or not we care to admit it, most of us assume that in some mysterious way it is our right to be able to apply the brakes when things don't go as we'd hoped. We organize all our comings and goings with brakes in mind, and so we fire up our engines outside the harbor entrance and drop our sails. This relieves us of the need for planning, which was the essence of the traditional boatman's day. With an engine running, we can proceed straight into the wind's eye and we can, within reason, stop at any time and at any angle to the wind. The need to rapidly assess a situation on the two premises that the boat cannot sail better than 50 degrees to the wind, and can only be stopped by the running down of her own momentum or some smart line handling, is thus removed. Unfortunately, a tremendous amount of job satisfaction goes out the porthole at the same time.

It is all too easy to rationalize our own shyness and to demean the achievements of our forebears with remarks such as, "Ah, but you see, the seas and the harbors were less crowded in *their* day."

Nonsense! Check out one of those old postcards depicting "Anstruther. The herring fleet comes in. 1898." Wall-to-wall sailing vessels is what we see. Furthermore, they are not short-keeled modern Bermudian sloops, which tack instantly through 90 degrees and which carry their way for 20 to 30 yards. Those are 40-ton luggers, needing a crew of ten to come about, and moving inexorably ahead for the length of a football field and more when luffed from a 6-knot reach.

To handle a boat under sail, we need to rethink some of our entrenched attitudes; we need, above all things, to understand about carrying way.

In this respect, as in most others, the real facts about a particular vessel can only be determined by experiment (see Chapter 7), but it is possible to make a good guess by considering her hull form. If she is a heavy-displacement craft, she will go a good deal farther than will a lightweight boat of the same length. Similarly, a 35-foot fishing smack packed with inside ballast will still be moving sedately ahead through a crosswind long after a flat-floored racing yacht half her length again has begun to blow sideways.

## The Standstill

Once committed to a head-to-wind standstill, a sailing yacht ceases to be under proper command. She cannot stay head-to-wind for any time at all unless her bow is tethered to something. The will to do so is just not in her, and she will fall off onto one tack or the other. If you're quick you can generally dictate which tack this will be, but even so, the boat will have to sail off downwind, then beat back up again, if she is to regain the position at which she stopped. It is therefore important to *keep way on* until you have arrived at the point where the boat is either to be anchored, or to be tied up to a dock or a mooring buoy.

If the boat does lose all way while head-to-wind before you are ready for her, she can be induced to fall onto the best tack for the circumstances by moving the helm so that the rudder points in the direction you want the stern to go. As she moves astern under the influence of the wind, the rudder will help kick her around. The job can be completed by backing the jib onto the same side as the rudder. If both these actions are taken just as the boat loses the last of her way, and not a moment sooner, she will spin around, and a happy recovery is assured. If you take action too late, the tack she adopts will be a lottery, since once she has started to swing, there will be little you can do to stop her.

The heart of every successful maneuver is planning and anticipation. Tactics and strategy are everything. Think yourself back into the minds of those men who had never used a wheel in anger, and retain a grip on your destiny by keeping the boat in a usable position relative to the wind for as long as it takes to work her sweetly to a standstill, just where you want her.

# 7

## SIZING UP THE SCENE

Before considering any maneuver under either power or sail, a correct assessment of what the wind is doing is required. It is also axiomatic that the tidal stream (or any other current) be correctly judged.

### True and Apparent Wind

The *true wind* is the breeze that is blowing across the deck of a vessel that is stationary relative to the ground. As soon as she begins to move, the effect of her passage through the airstream alters its apparent strength and direction. The resultant, or *apparent wind* may be significantly different from the true wind. Sails are set to the apparent wind that is blowing past them, but when planning your strategy it is usual to refer to the true wind, because this will decide such crucial questions as whether a buoy or harbor entrance can be made on the next tack, or whether it will be necessary to jibe at the next bend in the river.

A useful way to ponder the mystery of apparent wind is to consider an angler in a small motor-driven boat. He begins his day on a mooring buoy in a flat calm with his handy flag hanging limply from its staff. As he motors off at 6 knots through the still air, his passage creates an apparent headwind of 6 knots. Later in the day, back on his buoy, a light 6-knot breeze has kicked in. The angler decides he will motor in a downwind direction at 6 knots in search of a better

True and apparent wind

True wind 6 knots

True wind zero

Apparent wind 6 knots

True wind 6 knots

Apparent wind zero

Speed 6 knots

Apparent wind 12 knots

Speed 6 knots

Speed 6 knots

catch. In no time he has "caught up the wind." The air is flowing at 6 knots and he is motoring through the water at the same speed in the same direction. This means that his boat is no longer moving relative to the airstream, so the resulting apparent wind across his flag is zero.

If he gets sick of this and decides to head back for his mooring again, he will need to put on a sweater because he will now be logging 6 knots straight into a true wind of 6 knots. The natural headwind of his own progress will add to the true wind to create an apparent headwind of 12 knots.

Suppose he now veers off at 90 degrees to the true wind, what happens then? His flag makes a compromise between the two winds that it thinks are blowing. The flag is aware of the 6-knot headwind of the angler's motion, but it also feels the 6-knot true wind from directly abeam. The apparent wind is the result of these two. It will be coming from 45 degrees on the bow at about 8½ knots.

Whenever a boat is moving ahead, her apparent wind is always blowing from closer to her bow than is the true wind. The only exception is when the true wind is dead aft. Then, the speed of the boat's progress over the ground will diminish the apparent wind, while the direction of both remains unchanged.

## WIND ASSESSMENT

When a vessel is in motion, under either sail or power, the only wind which your senses (with the exception of your sight) can pick up is the apparent wind. The same is true of any instruments the boat may have, unless she has a computer feeding on not only the wind instruments, but also the ship's log. Even this will not give a strictly correct answer unless it is programmed to consider information about the tidal stream, which also affects apparent wind.

The apparent wind direction can be judged by reference to a burgee or a masthead "windex." It can also be very finely ascertained by feeling the wind as it blows over your ears. Face the wind, and carefully turn your head a few degrees from side to side, until you are sure that both ears are sensing the same amount of breeze. This method is extremely accurate, but if all else fails, there is always the good, old wet finger held optimistically aloft.

These methods also hold for sorting out the true wind direction when the boat is tied to the dock and going nowhere, but if you favor the electronic approach to Nature, you'll have to remember to switch off your computer at this point. If the tide is flowing past a through-hull log impeller, the computer will think the boat is moving at that speed relative to the breeze and will make corrections to what it thinks is the apparent wind. You'll just have to educate the thing by using the "off" switch.

So far, so good. But how do you sort out the true wind from the apparent when the boat is underway? In the absence of the computer (and when it comes to boat handling, the beast won't help you one jot), there are but two answers to this. The first is to make an informed guess based on the fact that the true wind will be farther aft than the burgee and your earlobes are suggesting. The second, and by far the most accurate method, is to use your eyes. There may be flags, smoke, etc., ashore, but compared with the gospel, these are as broken reeds. The place to see the true wind is ON THE WATER. Never mind the waves; look for the small, dark wind ripples. Unless it's really blowing, these are rarely above an inch high, but they are always visible, just as they are in a bowl of over-warm soup across which a well-mannered diner is surreptitiously blowing. Like the gourmet's cooling breath on the consommé, the wind on the sea is blowing at right angles to the ripples, and a right angle is easy to construct in the mind's eye. Don't look at the waves; they may be affected by many strange forces. Focus your gaze on the tiny ripples, and all will be revealed.

For some reason, many people find these blatant little signposts difficult to spot at first. Some see them straight away, others don't; but, once they are isolated from the rest of the visual data being pumped into the brain, they provide the solution to the question of true wind direction. So, if you don't find them obvious to start with, it's worth persevering.

## Assessing the Current

The only way to assess the direction of tide or current is to watch the water relative to some fixed object, such as a riverbank or a buoy. It's not unknown for a student skipper who has just received an over-dose of classroom theory to reply, when asked which way the tide is running past the dock to which he is moored, "Hang on, I'll just check the time of high water!"

Obviously, this is nonsense. Apart from anything else, the tide tables are at best merely predictions which may differ on the day from the facts, but even if they were "bomb-proof," it would still be a total waste of time to consult them.

Look over the side. Spit in the water if necessary. That's all that's required.

If you're approaching a stretch of water where the current is an unknown quantity from your present position, much can be learned from observing the lie of any moored or anchored vessels. Are they

Observing boats to determine wind/tide conditions

1. These boats indicate that either there is no appreciable current, or if there is one, that it is running WITH the wind.

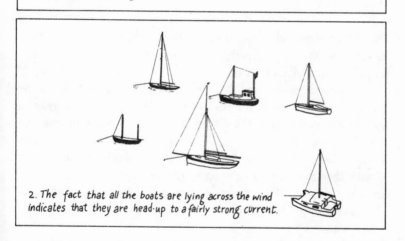

2. The fact that all the boats are lying across the wind indicates that they are head-up to a fairly strong current.

wind-rode? If so, there is either no stream or, if there is one, it's running with the wind. When the boats are not lying to the breeze, there is evidence of a current of some sort. Should every vessel be "head up" to the same direction, the stream is positively identified. If there is some discrepancy, this may be accounted for by the different hull forms of the boats. Deep, long-keeled boats will lie almost exclusively to the tide, except in strong crosswinds. Shallow craft such as cata-

3. This situation tells you that wind and current are in opposition, and that the current is relatively weak. The deep-draft cutter is probably lying to the stream, while the light-weight catamaran is obviously wind-rode.

marans or bilge-keeled yachts may well find themselves athwart the tide, and so on. An informed guess will give you enough information to rough out a plan of action.

Occasionally you'll be about to come alongside a dock on the bank of a river around the turn of the tide. Try as you may, you cannot judge or observe which way, if any, the stream is moving, but you don't want to risk coming down-tide onto the dock. When this state of affairs is upon you, the only thing to do is get the boat moving slowly, then steer her straight across the river toward the dock for a few seconds. She will be across any tide that is moving, and you'll be able to see what's going on.

## THE UP-TIDE APPROACH

Whenever a boat is being brought to a standstill "over the ground" where a current of any strength is running, it is of primary importance that, regardless of any considerations involving the wind, she approaches her mark *head-to-tide*.

There are two reasons for this. The first is obvious: It is simplicity itself to stop a boat when she is going up-current. Stopping her when she has the tide behind her will be extremely tricky under power and technically impossible under sail. The second reason is more subtle, and it is beautiful in its various spinoffs. When a boat in a strong tide is stationary over the ground, either on a mooring, or because she is about to pick one up, she is *still moving ahead through the water,* and she can therefore be steered. This opens up all sorts of delights when coming alongside (see Chapters 14 and 15), and if the knowledge is used properly, it makes mooring and anchoring far easier in a tideway than in slack water.

## USE OF RANGES (TRANSITS) IN TIDAL MANEUVERS

Prejudging the actual speed of a current is a nigh-on-impossible task. Fortunately, it is rarely necessary to do so, because the boat can

Transits

1.
Buoy 'on' with stationary cow. So long as they stay that way, the boat will arrive cleanly at her destination.

2.
Transit has opened, indicating that the boat has been allowed to slip down-tide. She must now either take up a new transit on the hill-top, or work back up-tide to her original friendly cow-line.

always be kept on line by sighting *ranges* (transits). Once you've decided which way you want the boat to travel over the ground for a particular part of a maneuver (usually the final approach), all you have to do is pick out any two fixed objects that line up behind your immediate destination. These will rarely be an "official" range; more often you will use a clump of grass on the riverbank in line with a gap in the hill, or maybe it'll be a mooring bollard "on" with the door handle of a motor vehicle, or the mooring buoy you are hoping to pick up sighted with a distant cow lying in a field.

What objects you choose is unimportant, but if you try to keep a boat going straight without any such help, you're going to need the judgment of Nelson to be in with even a starter's chance. Use a range, though, and your arrival at the point you are aiming for is guaranteed. Absolutely no skill is required. If the selected objects start to hint that you are being set "down," you steer more into the tide, power up the rig, or order up a few more revs. If they "open" the other way, you throttle back, let go the jibsheet, or steer a touch more across the tide. The range will tell you every time whether or not you've got it right. What's more, unlike tide tables, computers fed with flawed data, or your own subjective assessment, ranges will never tell you a lie.

# 8
## GENERAL HANDLING
## UNDER POWER

The art of handling a single-screw vessel is not to be underestimated, particularly when she is a deep-keeled yacht with a tiny propeller and a large amount of top-hamper to catch the wind. The number of times one hears remarks such as, "The old *Mud-Gobbler*'s a great sea-boat, but she's always been unpredictable under power," is nobody's business. Yet some people seem only to have to breathe on an awkward boat, and she will perform miracles for them. She will slide sideways into an apparently impossible berth; she will take way off in a straight line; she will even steer astern.

Why? What are the secrets to which these skippers are privy that lesser mortals never find? There is only really one, and it's called *prop-walk*. All the other tricks and techniques are merely an extension of boat handling under sail. Principles such as stalling at low speeds in a crosswind, the way the boat pivots about her center of lateral resistance, and such like, remain unaltered. The only thing different is that the boat is being urged to move not by sails, whose balance can be juggled almost infinitely so long as you don't try to sail straight into the wind, but by a propeller, which is firmly sited somewhere in the vicinity of the rudder.

## The Paddle-Wheel Effect (Prop-Walk)

Because it is turning like a mill, a propeller does not deliver its push as a smooth-edged gush of water sluicing out directly astern of the

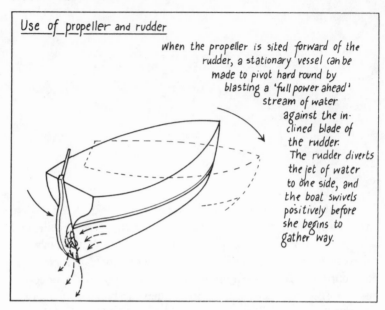

Use of propeller and rudder

When the propeller is sited forward of the rudder, a stationary vessel can be made to pivot hard round by blasting a 'full power ahead' stream of water against the inclined blade of the rudder. The rudder diverts the jet of water to one side, and the boat swivels positively before she begins to gather way.

boat. Instead, it sends out a vortex which not only drives the yacht ahead or astern, but also tends to push her stern to one side or the other.

When the vessel is making way in proper proportion to her engine revolutions, the propeller munches satisfyingly through the water, and these sideways effects are minimized. If the propeller is ideally sited forward of and reasonably close to the rudder, these effects are unlikely to be noticeable at all because the prop-wash will be running directly over the rudder blade, a tiny deflection of which at cruising speeds will be sufficient to neutralize them.

It is at the slow velocities required for close-quarters boat handling that prop-walk is most noticeable, because until the yacht is moving well, the propeller tends to thrash around without really grabbing the water. This aggravates its sideways tendencies, particularly when the engine is going in reverse because propellers are designed to push boats ahead, and few do both jobs equally well.

Another problem about going astern is that when the boat is not moving ahead, the rudder won't work very well, either. If the engine is thrown ahead and the rudder blade is put hard over, the resulting gush of water to one side of the boat will force the stern to cartwheel around in the opposite direction, assuming the propeller is sited forward of the rudder, as is usually the case. No such benefits are available when going astern. The propeller then becomes an inefficient shape which ends up shooting an inordinate amount of water out to whichever side of the boat its habit dictates. The rudder isn't much help, because rather than sending a great swirl of water over its blade as it does when going ahead, the propeller is shoving its rather messy vortex away in the opposite direction. The result is that heavy prop-walk is experienced.

## RIGHT- AND LEFT-HANDED PROPELLERS

The success or failure of all low-speed boat handling under power depends upon the knowledge and application of the following basic facts about the "handing" of propellers.

Most propellers are right-handed. This means that, looked at from aft, they turn clockwise when they are going ahead. Whatever

Propeller going astern

A propeller going astern, particularly in a stationary or slow moving vessel, generally expels far more water to one side than the other. The boat reacts accordingly and the stern 'prop-walks' to one side or the other.

name is attached to a propeller's behavior, however, what counts most to the skipper is what is going to happen when he puts the engine into reverse.

In the case of a right-handed propeller, the stern will walk to port if the propeller is turning in reverse, and rather less to starboard when going ahead. A left-handed propeller will have the opposite effect.

The strength of "propeller effects" varies greatly from boat to boat and depends on such things as keel form, rudder size and position, engine power, and the propeller itself. Generally speaking, if she has an engine of reasonable size and a decent propeller, a modern yacht with fin keel and spade rudder will be far less affected than a deep-keeled vessel. Why this should be remains a mystery, but true it usually is.

## DISCOVERING PROP-WALK

There are two ways to find out which way a boat is going to swing when the engine is put into reverse. The first method is useful if you are already underway and still don't know. Find yourself a stretch of calm water sheltered from any strong wind. If you can't escape

Discovering prop-walk: 1 on the dock

Engine running astern: more wash will appear on one side than the other. When she is free of the wall, you can expect her to swivel her stern AWAY from the side of most activity.
This boat's stern will swing to port when going astern, showing her to have a RIGHT-HANDED PROPELLER.

2. In open water

a. Boat moving slow ahead. Engine out of gear.

b. Astern is engaged.

c. Boat begins to swivel with her natural prop-walk, despite all that rudder can do.

the breeze, the exercise should be done with the boat motoring dead before the wind. Arrange for the boat to be moving slowly ahead with the engine out of gear. Now shift into reverse and give the engine about half throttle, making sure at the same time that you are steering firmly straight ahead. Watch the bow; in a few seconds you will see it cant to one side or the other. It will always be the same side, and the stern, of course, will be swinging in the opposite direction.

The second method has the benefit that it can be carried out while you are tied up. Start the engine, check the bow line and the stern spring, then put the engine into reverse, at about one-third throttle. Look over each quarter. You'll see far more water welling up on one side than the other, and you'll know that whenever you're going astern, your stern will try to swing away from the side with the greater disturbance.

## Making Use of Prop-Walk

Once you have established what your boat's natural preferences are, you will be unwise to ask her to do anything that is against her inclinations. Prop-walk is a powerful tool in the search for boat handling without blunders. If it is ignored, a potentially pliable vessel can become a perfect incubus. In Chapter 9 a number of exercises are considered for coming to grips with this feature of a boat.

## COMING ALONGSIDE

Whenever a boat is brought alongside under power, it is vital to consider which way she will swivel if it should prove expedient to put the engine into reverse to stop her. If she has a right-handed propeller, she is going to swing her stern to port. If all other things are equal, you should bring her in to the dock port-side-to, so as to encourage her to tuck her stern in neatly. You can then approach the dock at a sensible angle, confident in the knowledge that the yacht's propeller will continue to pull her in to the dock even after she has lost all her way. If you tried to dock starboard-side-to, the propeller would be fighting the rudder all the way and, since in the end the boat will be going too slowly for the rudder to have much effect at all, the propeller would win, resulting in an untidy arrival.

## THE SHORT TURN

Sometimes you need to turn a yacht in less distance than her natural turning circle. Occasionally she must manage in little more than her own length. The fin-and-spade boat is often able to turn very tightly indeed by virtue of her large rudder and small lateral area. Boats with more of their hulls in the water may find greater difficulty. For them, the answer lies in using prop-walk.

First, the boat is set up so that she is turning her favorite way, and has room enough to do so. The chosen spot is approached at a slow speed. When she has reached the right position, you put the helm hard over, and the boat begins to turn. Once she has gone as far as you are prepared to let her, the engine is put into reverse at half throttle *and the helm is left where it is.* The boat will continue to move slowly ahead, but the stern will prop-walk around, tightening the turn considerably. After a few seconds, the boat will stop making any forward progress, but will carry on swiveling. This will continue

The short turn

...you MUST set the turn up so you are swivelling WITH the propeller.

2. As the boat begins to move, run the engine half astern so that she checks her way and continues to prop-walk round...

3. As she gathers sternway, find neutral again, then give her another burst ahead.

4. And so on...

1. Helm hard over, full ahead burst against the rudder.

The secret of turning in your own length is to use propeller and rudder, but never to let the boat gather way.

as she starts to gather sternway. Most rudders will still be ineffectual, and if that is the case, leave the helm where it is; but if the rudder is found to be working, reverse it.

Before the boat has traveled any distance astern, put her out of gear again, make sure the helm is set so that she is steering into the turn once more, then go hard ahead. When the jet of water hits the rudder, the boat will swivel around firmly, but the effect will diminish as she begins to make headway. As soon as you see that her turn is widening, go astern again. Keep up the sequence until you are around.

The question of how long the engine should be allowed to remain either in forward gear or in reverse during this maneuver can only be decided after experiment, and considerable mechanical sympathy is required while it is being executed. It is all too easy to crash the gearbox from forward to reverse without the required one-second wait for the engine revolutions to die down. Gearboxes hate this sort of mistreatment, and the one thing you don't require during such a maneuver is to lose your drive, particularly in a strong crosswind with a line of expensive yachts immediately to leeward.

## Making Sternway

Steering a boat astern under power can be a nightmare. Some yachts (usually the fin-and-spade brigade) behave themselves perfectly, following obediently where their rudders are pointing. Others are unwilling, slow to catch on to what is required, and awkward when they do. A few are downright impossible.

What makes matters so difficult is that every boat has a certain critical speed astern, below which her rudder cannot overcome her prop-walk. Once you have found what this speed is, success is just a matter of knowing which way she will veer off before it is achieved, giving her room in which to do so, and then gritting your teeth and winding her up as quickly as you can. Control is usually established somewhere between 1 and 3 knots, but some boats can never go fast enough.

When your boat is making sternway, remember that the rudder is temporarily pivoted on the "wrong edge" and can easily take charge. This may result in personal injury if you get in the way of the tiller; it can also damage the rudder pintles, and if it causes you to "back up" into another yacht, it'll give you a nasty smack in the wallet. The only advice that can be offered is, "If you're going to hit a row of yachts, always pick the cheapest."

A yacht can often be helped to pull herself into line by giving her a sheer against the propeller before you start going astern. You can sometimes arrange this with lines if you are alongside, or by throwing the stern across with the rudder if you are maneuvering freely.

Beating the propwalk

This boat is to be driven astern between the piers. She is known to 'walk' her stern to port, so, before she starts to go astern, her stern is given a sheer to starboard. This allows her some space to pull herself back into line by the time she has enough way on to steer successfully.

swivelling round

½ knot    1½ knots    2 knots    2½ knots

Half of the yacht's tendency to swing will then be taken up before she hits the straight line, so she'll only go half as far beyond it before you gain steerageway.

Another action which can help to minimize the unpleasantness is to feed in the revs gradually. This avoids the thrashing propeller so productive of prop-walk, and helps the device to gain a grip on the water more rapidly. In the same vein, you can sometimes ease the situation while making sternway by throwing the engine out of gear for a while. This eliminates prop-walking altogether, and some boats will be ready to be steered back into line if it is done. Others, unfortunately, will remain unimpressed; once they've started to swing, it seems that nothing can stop them.

You'll only find out exactly where your own boat stands in this plethora of possibilities by experiment, but never forget that a sailing boat is highly unstable when she is underway astern. Propeller and rudder effects are only half the overall answer. On the day, windage might be just as important. The net effect of a sailing yacht's bare rig is generally centered on a point somewhat forward of her center of lateral resistance. If she also has a high bow, her tendency to blow "off" will be a strong one. If you're going to have to go astern in a crosswind, you'll need to assess whether all this windage will add to, or subtract from the boat's natural inclination to swivel in her usual way. Several "sternway" exercises are suggested in Chapter 9.

## Idiosyncrasies

There are other effects of the propeller about which it becomes increasingly difficult to generalize, but over which each and every boat will behave predictably, if individually. A typical example is what happens when a boat is moving ahead at 4 or 5 knots and you want to take way off by giving her a burst astern. Which side will her stern favor, if any? One would assume that it would simply go with the usual prop-walk, but in fact, it may well turn out to be the opposite. Once again, the answer can only be found by experiment.

There is enough theory below decks by now to tackle the business of boat handling in more practical terms. In the next chapter we'll look at a series of exercises and experiments which can be essayed in the privacy of a quiet anchorage well out of harm's way. Once those are under your belt, you'll have found out enough about your boat's behavior to be able to approach any maneuver, fast or slow, in harbor or at sea, with complete confidence that you do at least know what's going on.

# 9 AN ALTERNATIVE DAY'S YACHTING

There is absolutely nobody who can predict exactly what an unfamiliar boat will do in a given set of circumstances. An experienced skipper may be able to hazard a guess based on the boat's probable underwater shape, the power of her engine, the position of her masts, whether or not she sports a bowsprit, etc., but even he will need to experiment before he is sure.

Most professionals use a series of simple tests before laying a strange boat alongside a dock, particularly if she looks as though she may prove troublesome. In this chapter you will find a number of experiments that are useful in determining a vessel's behavior. There are also some exercises that are designed to sharpen up individual skills and perceptions. These will be of use to those who, due to other pressures, cannot spend as much time sailing as they'd like. If this is so in your case, it's well worth setting aside a day at the beginning of each season for no other purpose than to throw the boat around. It's a lot of fun, and it helps to free your mind from the fetters of that wretched motor-car that you drive every day of your life, but which does so much damage to your instinctive boating reactions by being more or less stuck to the road.

## Boat-Handling Exercises Under Power

### NATURAL ATTITUDE

It is always useful to know what angle a boat will adopt to the wind when floating free in calm water. Most sloops will settle at about 140 degrees from the wind. Once this has been ascertained, you'll know how hard the boat is trying to blow off her course on slow-speed approaches with the breeze at various angles from the bow. The closer she is to her natural attitude, the less unstable she'll be.

## CARRYING WAY

Try taking the power off at steady speeds of 2 knots, 3 knots, and 5 knots, and see how far she travels before she loses steerageway.

## STALLING SPEED

The best way to find out about this is to choose a windy day and a calm location. Motor straight into the wind, throw her out of gear, and see how far you can keep the boat moving before her head blows off to one side or the other. As soon as you begin to lose her, regain control with a burst of power against the rudder blade. How much power is needed, and for how long, to do no more than bring her back into line? This is a first-class exercise for developing a feel for your boat.

Now do the same thing with the wind at varying angles from the bow. Again, what you're after is to feel the developing stall through the tiller or wheel as lee helm becomes apparent. Practice giving the boat as little power as you can to beat the stall.

Next time you're approaching a berth with the wind blowing hard onto it, you'll be glad you've been working at this question. Your problem will be to keep the boat's head up while moving at the slowest speed, which is exactly what the exercise is about.

## PROP-WALK

In the previous chapter, we looked at the two main methods of discovering which way your boat prop-walks. Once you've worked it out, try a few 360-degree short turns. Nearly all yachts will spin around in less than two boat lengths. Is yours open to persuasion?

**Taking way off in a strong following wind.** One of the more obscure effects of prop-walk may crop up when you try to take way off the boat with a burst astern while she is carrying her way toward an objective. This is likely to occur when you are approaching a dock downwind in a stiff breeze with no room to turn around and come in "head up." A light-displacement yacht may blow down the breeze at 3 or 4 knots, and never stop at all. A heavier boat with more in the water will not be so unruly, but the same difficulty may still be experienced.

The odd thing is that above a certain speed, the propeller effect may prove less drastic than you expect. It can even contrive to reverse itself. You could be expecting the stern to throw to port as you carefully feed on the revs in reverse, when it suddenly veers off to starboard instead.

The reasons for this are deeply entrenched within the mysteries of laminar flow and cavitation, but, whatever the cause, you don't want to discover the phenomenon for the first time as you are approaching a narrow entrance with pricey gin-palaces stacked up at each side.

Try the boat out on a windy day. Then try her again on another occasion under similar circumstances. The only guarantee is that she'll be predictable in her apparent unpredictability. If she isn't, there has been a subtle change in the conditions, and you haven't noticed.

## MAKING STERNWAY

As was the case with prop-walk, we've already considered the general "ins and outs" of moving astern. The time to put the matter to the test is now, when there is plenty of room.

First try going astern upwind. This is going to provide by far the greatest chance of success, because the boat's greater windage forward will keep her bow "down" so that she can proceed in a straight line. Then try maneuvering across the breeze "against the propeller," then go in the opposite direction with the prop-walk helping to counteract the wind. Finally, see if the boat can be persuaded to go astern dead downwind. If it's a fresh afternoon, she won't like that at all, but at least you'll discover whether or not it's possible.

If the whole business has gone smoothly, you could round things off by attempting a figure-of-eight as a final *tour de force*. If this works as well, you will know no more terrors as you "back out" of your marina berth under the neighbors' ghoulish gaze.

## Boat-Handling Exercises Under Sail

### CLOSE REACHING AND WIND AWARENESS

First, select a sensible sail combination for the conditions. This should be fairly modest but capable of producing a reasonable amount of drive.

Once you are content that your rig will give efficient performance without high drama, a good starting point is to lay the boat beam-on to the wind and let off the sheets. See if she will lose way completely or if she continues to creep ahead. You will probably find that the leech of the mainsail will not spill the last of its wind; if so, release the center vang. This will make a big difference.

If the boat still won't lose all her way beam-on, bring her steadily up toward the wind, and find out how close she must be before she will stop. The angle she is making to the true wind at the time she finally stalls is the "low" side of her "close-reaching window."

Now haul in a few feet of mainsheet so as to get her moving in this direction. Sail her with as low a boat speed as you can manage, spilling wind all the time, ever higher to windward until she just won't take any more. As she stalls, her head will fall off the wind. See how effectively you can control the tendency by sheeting in the mainsail, but note carefully the closest angle to the wind at which the boat will sail slowly. That is the "high" side of the close-reaching window.

Now that the window of best control has been defined, you know with certainty that so long as you can maneuver to put your desti-

## Exercises for making sternway

wind

1. This one is easy, because the boat's natural tendency is to lie with her head somewhat down-wind.

2. If her propwalk takes her stern to port, this one is also no problem. As her prop tries to swing the bow to windward, the breeze blows it off again, and the boat is controllable.

4. In certain boats this may prove impossible in a strong breeze.

3. In this case the stern is tending to swing to port as the wind blows the bow off to starboard — very difficult to handle.

## The close-reach window

wind

45°-50°

THE CLOSE REACH WINDOW

75°-80°

Most boats will be able to spill wind and retain control between 50 and 80° from the wind.

To windward of 50° she will not generate enough drive from her flogging sails to move ahead. Downwind of 80°, she will not be able to slow down, because her mainsail will be full of wind.

nation somewhere between its low and high edges, you can make an approach with absolute confidence.

If there are moorings in your chosen exercise area, pick one at random and try to place your boat in such a position that when you steer toward it, your boat is on a perfect close reach. Approach it, but don't bother to pick it up; just see if you can stop alongside. Then select another and do it again. And again, and again. This is great training for the wind awareness that is the root of all maneuvering under sail.

## BOAT BALANCE AND PIVOTING

Set the boat up so that she is stationary, with the wind more or less abeam and both sails spilling. Let go the helm. Now pull in the mainsheet, and see how far and how hard she luffs.

Repeat the exercise using the jibsheet instead. Does she bear away? If so, how much, and for how long?

Now note the direction of the wind by observing the water. Sail the boat on a reach, with the true wind just abaft the beam and the sails correctly trimmed. When she is moving well, see if she will tack without touching the mainsheet. Many boats will do this adequately, but it may be a different story in half a gale and a steep sea. Do it again, only this time haul in hard on the mainsheet as the boat comes to the wind, keeping the sail drawing all the time. The difference may surprise you.

## HEAVING TO

Heave the boat to by tacking her and leaving the jibsheet fast. Don't forget to put the helm "down" to leeward as equilibrium is being reached (a wheel will, of course, be wound "up" to windward, but the correct term is still "helm down"). Once the boat has settled, play with the sheets and see if you can induce her to point up or down by altering the balance of her rig.

Having mastered the technique of heaving to, it is worth trying to persuade the boat to "fore reach" at speed. In order to do this, the jib is sheeted onto the yacht's midline by utilizing *both jibsheets,* and the mainsail is sheeted into something like a close-reaching attitude. Once the boat is well underway, the helm is allowed to swing free (if the boat has a wheel-steering mechanism that will not spin from one side to the other, the wheel is locked around about amidships). The boat should now sail herself ahead on a very close reach. When she is moving well, try easing one sheet, then another, and note what it does to the yacht's heading relative to the wind.

Not only can this technique be of great use in short-handed and hard-weather sailing (see Chapter 16), it is a wonderful self-training aid for a crew to learn about sail balance in general, and their own craft in particular.

## LOSING WAY BY STALLING SAILS

Experiment to find out how effectively the boat is slowed down by oversheeting the sails, both on a reach and downwind. Check what this is doing to the helm balance, particularly in the case of the mainsail. You may find that the boat becomes hard to steer if it's a breezy day.

And so on. See what you can come up with for yourself to solve any points of interest that have arisen.

## THE TRIANGLE

As soon as you've given yourself an insight into the boat's capacity to help herself maneuver, you can increase the interest by arranging a three-cornered course to sail around. One buoy should lie approximately to windward of another, while a third, the wing mark, is placed out to one side so that the three form an equilateral triangle. The distance up the windward leg can be anything you like, but 200 yards is ideal.

When you set up your course, you'll need to be creative with what Nature or the local yacht club mooring committee have provided. With luck, you'll find a couple of buoys that will do duty as two corners of the triangle. For the third, you can always lay your kedge with a fender tied to the end of the rode.

Having set up the course, start working around it from the lee-

The exercise triangle

wind

windward mark

wing mark

leeward mark

200m.

ward buoy, concentrating on really *sailing* the boat. Make lots of tacks as sweetly as you can; ditch the mainsheet as you bear away around the top mark; jibe tightly and without fuss at the wing; trim immaculately down the reach, then harden up *all* the sheets as you swing around the leeward mark to start again.

When you've got the idea, see if you can manage it without passing more than a boat length from the buoys; then, half a boat length. As soon as you've achieved that, you can time yourself and start a serious competition. After an hour, you and your crew will be sweating hard, but you'll have learned more about sailing than most folks pick up in a season.

When you're confident that you can do it as fast as an America's Cup crew, see how slowly you can manage, without ever losing control or hitting a mark. That'll stop you from feeling too pleased with yourself. . . .

## THE MAN-OVERBOARD GAME

This is the best exercise in the world for teaching wind awareness and the sense of tactics vital for successful boat handling under sail. There are many different ways of maneuvering a boat back to a person in the water. This is only one of them. It also happens to be about the best, but *only if you're a good sailor*. We'll go more deeply into this whole subject in a later chapter. For now, it is an exercise and nothing else.

- Get the yacht moving fast on any point of sailing, and throw the dan-buoy (or a bucket and a fender tied together) over the side.
- Detail someone to watch it, lest you should become disoriented and lose sight of it.
- Immediately sail the boat away, properly trimmed, on a beam reach.
- When you've enough room to maneuver, either tack or jibe. Bear in mind that tacking will take you further upwind. Jibing will lose you ground. Either may be what you want.
- Steer the boat toward the dan-buoy, and see whether or not she is on a CLOSE REACH within the limits you have defined for her. (Don't forget to dump the center boom vang, if necessary.)
- If she *is* on a close reach, lose way and slowly approach the dan-buoy.
- If she's "below" a reach (i.e., to leeward of the desired heading, or too hard on the wind), make all the ground you can close-hauled, "above" the target, before bearing away and spilling wind on your final, close-reaching approach. Failure to do this will result in the boat stalling into the windward sector as soon as you try to slow down.
- If she's "above" the desired heading (you'll know this because you won't be able to persuade the mainsail to spill wind properly), you must bear away sharply, run downwind for a few yards, then steer once more for the buoy, taking another look at your angle to the wind.
- The reason why you sailed so far away from the dan-buoy on the initial beam reach was in order to have enough sea-room to execute either of these last two maneuvers, if they should be required. Do not waste that ground through indecision.

The man overboard game

This is the finest exercise of all for practising all the elements of 'free-sailing' boat handling, but wind awareness is the essence of the exercise throughout the operation. keep checking not only apparent wind but true wind on the water.

wind

gybe

close reach

The pick-up

c. As the boat arrives at the objective, she is luffed ALMOST head to wind as she begins to stall. This will encourage her to drift to leeward down onto the buoy as the last of her way comes off.

a, b.
Final approach on a close reach, speed controlled by spilling wind.

- To reiterate: As soon as you have tacked or jibed, steer for the buoy and let all sheets right off. You will be in one of three situations: If you are well above the closehauled line but all your sails will spill wind, you have it made. If the mainsail *won't* spill, you must bear away smartly before heading back up for the buoy again and reassessing your chances. If you are too near to being closehauled, power upwind for a few yards before bearing away onto your final approach. Whatever you do, there is no time to lose.

- As for picking up the buoy, you'll discover that if you stop to windward of it with the breeze well out on your weather bow, the stalling boat will slide down toward it, particularly if you put the helm right to leeward to luff off the last of her way. You'll then be able to pick it up amidships. Watch out for the flogging jibsheet, though. If you've a roller genoa, furl it before you go out on the deck.

Finding that close reach in the heat of the moment requires judgment of a moderately high order. Don't be disheartened if this exercise seems hard going. Try it again after a few months, but if you are in any doubt, stick to one of the other man-overboard methods if there is an emergency in the meantime.

Don't ever kid yourself, however. Until you can do this, you can't really sail. An able boat handler can pull it off tidily at any time, day or night (with a floating light), in fair weather or foul, in any boat within reason.

That's something well worth aiming for, but without practice, you'll never get there.

# *10* MOORINGS

Mooring buoys are like hats: They come in all sizes and fulfill a multitude of functions. Some are small, others are large; some are inconspicuous, others stand out like an Ascot bonnet. Many are designed purely for lightweight use on summer afternoons, but some offer security in the worst of winter gales.

When you pick up a strange mooring, deciding what you've got is the first priority. If the mooring has been set by the harbor or yacht club authorities, their representative will be the first to tell you if it is unsuitable for your vessel. Otherwise, unless you can find a reliable local who knows the mooring's recent history, you'll have to trust your own judgment on such questions as whether or not it is man enough for a boat of your tonnage, and if it has seen any maintenance since Eve ate the Apple. As in all things maritime, however, common sense will not let you down. Checking a mooring for clues as to its intended use, its frequency of tenure, and the like is a fascinating pastime.

When you are approching a mooring, you should assess in plenty of time what will be the means of securing your bow to it. Does it have a pickup buoy to beckon your boathook? If so, then in all probability it will also supply a chain or rope pennant of some description to make fast to your foredeck cleat or samson post.

If the mooring has no pickup buoy, you must be ready with a length of line of your own, *ready* being the watchword. You'll probably opt for rigging this line as a slip-rope (i.e., through the ring in the buoy and back to the boat again) to begin with, because the helmsman may not make life easy for the troops on the foredeck and the last thing they'll want is to be tying knots with their cold fingers. You'll need up to 20 feet of line for the initial job; no more. Don't have a large heap of rope all over the foredeck waiting to foul on something, or be dropped over the side into the propeller. If your rope is long, make the bight fast on one cleat so you've 20 feet of free end to work with. Lead this out through the fairlead, over the roller, or whatever your boat provides; you are then ready to pass it through the ring on the buoy, bring it back aboard, take up the slack, and make fast.

When the slip-rope is on, you can organize matters to suit the occasion. If you're stopping for lunch on a calm day, just lie to the slip-rope. If you're staying overnight, by far the best thing is to shackle your anchor chain to the buoy, but leave the slip-rope on for handling purposes. You can pull most buoys right up to the stemhead with the slip-rope while you shackle on the cable. If you wire the shackle, you are as safe as the buoy is. There are just two problems.

The first annoyance with "chaining up" is that the noise may drive you to the false comfort of the medicinal bottle; the second is that if you need to leave in a hurry, a wired shackle may prove less than ideal.

The alternative way to secure to a buoy with a ring is to use a stout line secured with a *round turn* and a *long bowline*. The round turn is to kill any chafe, and the long bowline is used so that you can reach the knot without having to adopt too obsequious a pose. The slip-rope is left on for handling purposes.

## LASSOING A BUOY

This is a technique for taking an initial hold on a mooring buoy that has no pickup and which, for one reason or another, you feel you are likely to miss with the boathook. A length of line (which must be of a non-floating variety) is made fast on both sides of the bow with the bight running around the boat's stem, outside everything. How long the bight should be will depend upon the vessel and the circumstances, but about 20 feet is a good starting point. When the boat has been brought as near as she is going to come to the buoy, the bowman lobs the bight over it. The rope then sinks "around" the buoy and tightens up as the yacht falls away. The arrangement is highly impermanent, but once the yacht has been secured in this manner she can be pulled up to the mooring at leisure and made fast more conventionally.

It sounds improbable, but it works nearly every time.

## Mooring Under Power

### CALM CONDITIONS

Approaching a mooring where no tide is running and there is no significant breeze, is ease itself. Just remember that if you rush at the job and then gun the engine astern, you're going to prop-walk the bow away from the buoy. So, take it easy.

As in all mooring operations, it pays to decide early which side of the bow you will lay onto the buoy. Groping over the top of the pulpit is not the way to pick up the buoy. It is far simpler for the boathook operator to grab the mooring if you stop the boat with the buoy somewhere between the stemhead and the main shrouds. Tell the crew which side, and all will be peace.

### STRONG WINDS

If it's blowing hard, you'll have to approach the buoy from downwind. Bear in mind, however, that as the boat slows down, she's likely to stall. If she's head-to-wind, you may experience problems keeping her head up at the end of the operation, which will result in an unseemly scrabble over the weather guardrails to grab the buoy as it disappears to windward. It is preferable in these sort of conditions to finish your approach with the wind 10 degrees or so on one side of the bow, and choose the lee side to lay against the buoy (assuming the buoy is of a soft material). Then, as you slow down, the boat will be certain to stall into the buoy rather than be running the risk of falling away from it.

If the buoy is made of steel, you won't want to bash your topsides on it, so the only answer is a straight-upwind approach. Be aware of the fact that the boat will blow away sideways soon after she's stopped. If you've overrun the buoy at all, make sure that you stall away from it after the rope is on. The metal mooring is an ideal candidate for the lasso method of initial attachment.

## STRONG TIDES

Given that you have arranged for an up-tide approach, this is by far the easiest condition in which to moor. There are no problems of blowing around once you've lost way because, relative to the water, you're still moving. So, of course, is the mooring buoy. All you have to do is to "nail" the buoy onto an object behind it when you are still some distance away on your final approach. It doesn't matter if you are coming partly across the tide. Once this range is established, the boat has only to be kept on it for success to be assured. As with all pickups, decide which side of the bow you'll put the buoy on; then, when you are right up with it, come head-to-tide with the buoy placed as advertised.

When mooring in a tideway, it is important to keep the boat moving through the water until the crew have completed their task. The job isn't finished until they have called out the "All fast." If you allow the boat to sheer across the stream while they are still working, they may be unable to hang on. Maintain your station carefully by using new ranges: one pair ahead of you, and one pair abeam. Keep both of these "on," and you'll be as solidly placed as the mooring itself. The crew will have an easy time making fast, and they'll never know why.

## WIND ACROSS TIDE

This is always the interesting one, and there is no "off-the-peg" answer that guarantees results. Generally, however, tide will prevail over wind in the case of a deep-drafted sailing vessel. Look at the way any other moored boats are lying. If you approach at a similar angle to craft like your own, you won't go far wrong. Just remember to pick a range behind the buoy and *keep it "on."*

In many a circumstance, the lethal pickup buoy can cause a great deal of trouble if you allow the boat to sail between it and the main mooring. This must be avoided at all costs, especially if the boat is a fin-keeler. The pickup pennant will take full advantage of any opportunity you give it to insinuate itself between keel and rudder.

### SLIPPING A MOORING UNDER POWER

When you are leaving a mooring under power, it is important to be sure not to foul your propeller on either the mooring itself or, more likely, the pickup pennant. The simplest way to be certain is to let the boat blow away from the buoy before engaging the gears. If there isn't the wind for this, you can always go astern.

Sometimes, the proximity of neighboring vessels, or the state of wind and tide, dictate that you must leave by going ahead past the buoy. If so, you have two choices: You can give the boat enough of a sheer to clear the mooring, and then swing the stern away from it as you go by—always remembering that it is your propeller the rope is looking for, and that the boat pivots around her keel. The other method is for the crew to walk aft along the side deck, still hanging on to the mooring as you motor away. When he is standing on the quarter, he releases it, ensuring that it falls well clear.

## Mooring Under Sail

### NO TIDE

Mooring under sail in slack water is by far the most difficult of the various possibilities. The reason is that, unlike any situation where there is a tide running, the boat must be brought to a virtual standstill at exactly the right spot.

The surest way of doing this is to approach the mooring on a close reach, going as slowly as you possibly can (see Chapters 6 and 9). The aim should be to stall the boat just as the buoy is nudging the

Picking up a mooring under sail – slack water

Way is lost as the boat approaches the buoy on a close reach. The last of her motion is 'luffed off' so that the boat stops with the buoy against one side of her bow.

wind

lee bow, but a neater result will be obtained if, instead of sailing directly toward the buoy itself, you close reach toward a point a few yards to leeward of it; then, just before you are dead downwind of the buoy, luff up to it, taking off the last of your way as you do so. Make sure that the buoy is on the designated side of the bow, though, or the boathook platoon won't thank you.

On most boats you'll be better off doing this under jib and main, but if you are fortunate enough to have a yacht that will close reach under main alone, it may pay you to take the jib down in good time. The foredeck crowd will have less unpleasantness if you do. They don't like having their ears boxed by the brass-bound clew of a headsail, even though the close-reach approach does keep this to a minimum.

The roller jib scores high points here. You can have just enough jib drawing to maintain drive; then, when you are confident that you don't need the sail anymore, roll it away.

## WIND WITH TIDE

The only difference between this and the no-tide situation is that you'll have to sight a range in good time to be sure you are not set

Picking up a mooring under sail- wind with tide

wind

close-reach heading

transit line

tide

Track slides across to buoy

When the wind and tide are together, the approach must be made from further upwind than if there were no tide. The secret of success is the transit.

below the buoy. You may find it more difficult to pick a close reach, however. The dynamics of the situation will speak for themselves, but remember that because you are being swept downwind by the tide, you will do well to start from "higher up" than you would otherwise have done. Don't be too concerned about overdoing this; it's easy enough to lose ground when you are nearer the buoy by luffing into the tide, or spilling wind to slow down. If you judge things correctly, you will slide across the tide onto the mooring, which will be picked up on your lee bow.

Don't forget that as soon as the buoy is hooked, you must steer straight into the tide so that the hands can bring it aboard without having to fight the boat as she sheers across the stream. Once your way is off, you can't get it back as you could under power, so you must make use of what you have left after luffing to give the crew the easiest time you can.

## WIND ACROSS TIDE

If the wind is forward of the beam, but broader than closehauled when you are stemming the tide toward the buoy, this is the easiest state of all. You are, of course, on a good, old close reach, so you can go as fast or as slow as you like. Since you will never have to go any slower than the speed of the tide, you probably won't have to come anywhere near stalling speed. You can just nudge up toward the mooring and keep sailing on the spot while the crowd up forward make you fast.

On the other hand, if you find that, when you are stemming the tide, the breeze is abaft the beam, you have an entirely different situation. You are into a "wind-against-tide mooring."

## WIND AGAINST TIDE

It is of paramount importance that anyone who is intending to sail onto a mooring, up to an anchorage, or alongside a dock, has a working definition of "wind against tide." Without one, all sorts of marginal situations such as the one described in the previous paragraph will be misjudged, and chaos will be the result.

The definition is simple: Assess the direction your boat will be headed when she is at rest on the mooring. If there are other moored boats handy, so much the better. Look at them for the answer. Then ask yourself the crucial question, "When my yacht is in that attitude, will my mainsail be capable of spilling wind, or will it be pressed

*Picking up a mooring under sail – wind against tide*

In any wind against tide pick-up, it is VITAL that the mainsail is dropped (1). Speed on the down-wind, up-tide approach is then controlled by using the jib sheet (2,3,), or by dropping the sail altogether (4).

against the shrouds?" If the answer is, "Yes, it will spill wind," you do not have a wind-against-tide situation. If the answer is "No, it won't," or even "Hmmm. . . . ," then you have.

The only way of stopping a boat relative to a mooring buoy is to approach up-tide, just as you would under power. If this means your main can't be allowed to flog out its wind, there is but one solution: Drop it, and pick up the mooring downwind under jib only, checking your way with the sheet (see Chapter 6). Because the breeze is abaft the beam, you don't require the mainsail for upwind drive. The whole operation is a piece of cake, and if you try to do the job by any other method (luffing up across the tide, for example), misery, humiliation, and broken heads from the resulting jibes on the buoy will be your just reward.

The wind-against-tide pickup is notably sweet for the foredeck gang because the headsail is blowing away from them (or being rolled up as required) and the driver can hold the boat beside the buoy at exactly the speed of the tide while they fumble away to their hearts' content.

## SLIPPING A MOORING UNDER SAIL

This presents no problems if you adhere to the above principles for deciding whether or not to set the mainsail on the buoy. If you reckon it's wind-against-tide, you'll have to sail away under headsail. When you've got room, you can bring the boat onto a close reach and hoist the main. There is no need to luff head-to-wind for this; it only makes life difficult. So long as the sail can spill wind, it can always readily be hoisted. The same applies to dropping it.

If you are surrounded by other boats and you are hoisting main and jib, you must consider from first principles what may go wrong. Remember that after you have dropped the mooring, the boat will slide sideways some distance before she overcomes her stall and begins to drive forward. If you intend to leave closehauled, this will be important, because, left to her own devices, your boat may slide all the way into the next boat. Should you decide that, because of this, you won't be able to pass clear ahead of your neighbor, you'll

Slipping from crowded moorings:
Disaster

Boat A elects to sail out to windward, but forgets
that she will start off in a stalled state. She has not
gathered enough way for her keel to grip properly before she slams into boat B.

Triumph!

This time, boat A goes for
the safer option of bearing
away astern of boat B.

However, to succeed she must not
forget the following: ● The mainsail
must be depowered by overhauling the
sheet and dumping the vang (1,2)
● The jib must be backed and the HELM
REVERSED as she drops the mooring (1). If she
keeps the helm reversed through stage 2, it will continue to assist. ● Only when the
main begins to draw is the jib sheeted in and the boat steered away around B's stern.

have to bear away hard immediately after you've slipped the mooring. Without good handling, the boat may not want to cooperate.
The rudder won't be working right away, so if you are to avoid a
collision, you'll need to steer with the sails (see Chapters 2 and 5).
Overhaul the mainsheet to the knot, dump the boom vang, back the
jib, and the boat will bear away so fast she'll surprise even herself.

# 11 ANCHORING

## The Theory of Anchoring

The art of anchoring used to be well understood by everyone who went down to the sea in cruising yachts. In recent years, however, marinas and visitors' moorings have proliferated so that for many, though by no means all of us, anchoring has become an unusual activity. The result is that a knowledge of the rudiments of anchoring has dropped down the list of the sailor's priorities.

Consider the case of the yacht *Dumbo* as she comes swanning into Snugbury Bight one quiet Sunday lunchtime. She finds herself a hole amongst the fleet of moored and anchored lotus-eaters, and brings herself to a standstill. Macho Mike lumbers up to the foredeck and throws open the bow locker with a crash. He drags out an apology for an anchor, peers myopically at it to see which way up it goes, then heaves it over the bow. By a miracle of chance he has contrived to lead it through the pulpit and over the roller, so that an indeterminate length of chain is able to follow it noisily into the limpid depths of the bay. Mike snubs the cable when he thinks the anchor has touched the bottom; then, without a glance at the outside world, he climbs back aft and goes below. A cork pops, and sounds of revelry filter up through the hatch.

After an hour or so, a somewhat belated seabreeze kicks in. The yachts in the bight swing gently so that their sterns are toward the beach. Not so the *Dumbo*. Her head falls off impotently, and away she goes, sideways, to pile up on the landing under the patio bar of

*Anchoring*

The weight of chain cable allows a shorter scope to be effective.

rope >5×depth

chain 3×depth of water

the Snugglers Arms, where the lunchtime drinkers get good value for the price of their beer.

You've probably made a mental list by now of all the things Macho Mike did wrong. Poor *Dumbo!* She never stood a chance, because her skipper paid no attention to any of the basic facts of how an anchor works. These are as follows:

- An anchor performs its function by digging into the sea-bed and taking a firm hold.
- It will only do this if it is laid on the bottom and then pulled positively but carefully along.
- In order to enable an anchor to work itself into a holding position, a pull with a large horizontal component is required. This means that if you are anchoring with chain, a length equivalent to three times the depth of water must be allowed to run out (this is known as a *scope* of 3 : 1). Should you elect to use a nylon rode with a short length of chain on the anchor end of it, you will need five times the depth of water to achieve the same result. The reason for the difference in scope is that a length of chain in the water droops down into a curve called a *catenary* by means of its own weight. The chain between the nylon rode and the anchor, which should be at least 10 feet in length, serves to assist the horizontal component of the pull; it also provides a vital anti-chafe device against abrasion by the sea-bed.
- The scope that is required to enable an anchor to bury itself also

ensures that the hook stays put when the load comes on. It is therefore doubly important when laying chain that the boat is, if possible, induced to move steadily away from the anchor, so that when her weight is brought up by the ground tackle, it will dig in the anchor. If a pile of chain is dropped on the bottom, the boat may lie satisfactorily to it until the system is tested, but once anything serious is asked of the anchor, it will fail because it was never properly "set," as was the case with the *Dumbo.*

- Somehow or other, the yacht must actively work her anchor into the bottom. If you are intending to go off watch, it really isn't good enough to leave the ironmongery lying around down there and hope for the best. You must KNOW that you are properly anchored.
- Both during the anchoring process and afterwards, the crew should use ranges to make sure that the yacht is not going anywhere.

## Choosing a Place to Anchor

Since this is a book about sailing and boat handling, rather than navigation and general seamanship, there is no need to dwell at any length on this question. Common sense should dictate whether a bay, river, or roadstead will be sheltered, and be likely to remain so for the length of your intended stay. In general terms, one is looking for protection from the sea rather than the wind, since it is waves and pitching which usually pull an anchor out of the bottom. If you have chosen a site with good holding ground (firm mud or clay is best, though sand can work well also) and have set your anchor well, the wind should not present any problems, unless it blows up in truly horrendous proportions.

If a hard blow is expected, it's well worth selecting an anchorage which offers the potential for laying an enormous scope of cable. We are not going to consider all the possible ways of laying out extra anchors; that is a subject about which books can be and have been written. Suffice it to say that a single large, well-designed anchor dug well in on 10:1 scope of chain cable is as near to being an ideal safety net as you are ever likely to get.

## DEPTH CONSIDERATION

You must find somewhere to anchor in which there is plenty of water to float the boat *all around her swinging circle,* at all states of the tide. Within those criteria, the shallower the water the better, because this will allow you to use more scope if you need it, or less cable out of the locker (and less work for you) if you don't.

## SWINGING ROOM

When you enter an anchorage with even one other boat in it, you can bet your favorite bower to a rusty grappling iron that she'll have

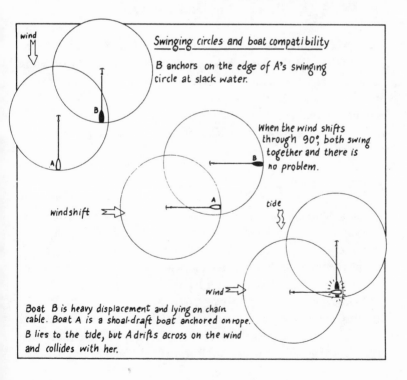

wind ⬇

<u>Swinging circles and boat compatibility</u>

B anchors on the edge of A's swinging circle at slack water.

When the wind shifts through 90°, both swing together and there is no problem.

windshift ⇒

tide ⬇

wind ⇒

Boat B is heavy displacement and lying on chain cable. Boat A is a shoal-draft boat anchored on rope. B lies to the tide, but A drifts across on the wind and collides with her.

hogged the best place. Well, tough luck, old son. It's first come, first served. That's the ancient custom of the sea. So, you'll just have to accommodate yourself somehow.

When an anchorage is crowded, you might have to anchor inside someone else's swinging circle. If you do, try to pick a boat with similar characteristics to your own so that you'll swing together and stay out of each other's way. A racing trimaran will behave so differently at anchor from a heavy-displacement cruising yacht that the only thing they'll have in common is that both are afloat. Bedfellows don't have to be as strange as those two in order to take their partners for the "Edgartown Waltz," however. Whatever the next-door boat, if she is using rope and you are favoring chain, forget it! The two are as incompatible as a snail and a bumblebee.

## Anchoring Under Power

One of the improvements in life brought about by the universal auxiliary engine is that one can now be sure the anchor is holding before the matter becomes critical. As we shall see, a certain amount can be done in this department under sail alone, but if the wind is light there may be a question mark remaining which will only be resolved by soaked pajama-clad sufferers dragged from their bunks by a sudden midnight squall.

### ANCHORING WITH CHAIN

The process of anchoring under power is delightful in its simplicity. The yacht is headed up to the wind, or the tide if there is any. The anchor is let go just as you begin to make sternway over the ground. Where there's a tide, it may take the boat away for you. If the water is slack, it will be necessary to go astern under power.

While the boat is moving away from her anchor, cable is *laid* (not dumped) steadily so that it lies in a straight line between boat and anchor. When enough cable has run out, it is snubbed and the engine is put out of gear so that the momentum of the boat begins to dig in

Laying an anchor

1. Anchor is let go.

2. Boat moves off astern, laying cable along the bottom as she goes.

3. When chosen scope has run out, cable is snubbed and boat digs in her anchor using the last of her way, then the engine is run astern.

4. Boat lies securely to her anchor.

the anchor. Now comes the clever bit. The hand on the foredeck watches the cable carefully. As soon as it looks as though the boat is about to be pulled ahead by the weight of the chain being held off the bottom, he signals the skipper to go astern. The engine is now put in reverse at half throttle, and the boat will pull steadily on the cable. This serves two purposes: It gives the anchor the horizontal pull that it needs to work itself into the sea-bed; and it gives the crew confidence that if the anchor will hold with that amount of power on it, it is unlikely to be plucked out by anything the coming night has to offer.

While the engine is in reverse, the foredeck boss should watch the cable to see if it "ducks"; this will indicate some movement on the sea-bed. You would expect the cable to bounce a little initially, while any final kinks are pulled out, but once the situation has stabilized, the cable shouldn't move at all. Some people like to put a hand on it and feel what it's doing. Meanwhile, the skipper should be sighting ranges abeam to make sure the boat is not creeping astern. If she is, he can try a little more scope. If that doesn't work, he'll have to pull up the hook and have another go. The anchor may well break the surface all fouled up with kelp, or with one of its flukes stuck jauntily into an old beer can, bucket, or chamber pot.

The business of digging in the anchor should be done with the stealth of a cat burglar. If you go blasting off astern at 4 knots, snub your cable, then expect the anchor to stop you, you deserve to be unlucky. If the anchor holds, your problems are surely at an end, but it is far more likely to plough a shallow furrow along the bottom and never get a grip. The anchor must be worked into the mud by a combination of sensitivity and strength. Having got the knack, you'll cruise around the world and back without ever dragging anchor.

## ANCHORING WITH LINE

The only difference between the processes of anchoring with chain and anchoring with line is that when you are using rope it becomes even more vital that you dig the anchor in. This is because, unlike chain, rope has no damping properties other than those inherent in its natural elasticity. Each time the boat surges about on a gusty night, she tugs at her anchor, while the yacht on chain cable may well do no more than lug a bight across the sea-bed. When you are confident that the anchor has a good hold, pour on plenty of power and make sure. Then you'll sleep soundly. You can even take a drink if you fancy it. Just keep an eye on two or three sets of ranges to make sure that you are staying where you should be.

It is vital that all anchor rodes be of nylon manufacture. Not only is this the strongest rope available, it stretches an improbable amount before it comes anywhere near its breaking strain. This damps to a certain extent the yacht's natural tendency to snub her anchor.

## Weighting the Cable and Laying Out a Second Anchor

Occasionally, conditions in an anchorage become so hectic that even with the maximum possible scope laid out for the bower anchor, you require still more holding power. The first action is to lower a weight down the cable in order to depress the catenary. The weight must be of at least 60 pounds to do any good on even the smallest yachts, and care should be taken to guard against chafe if you are anchored on rope.

It used to be possible to purchase weights ready-made for this purpose, and beautiful items they were. In these enlightened times, however, we must make them up for ourselves.

The benefit of deploying a weight is really two-fold: Not only does it serve to hold down the cable and ensure that the anchor pulls in a horizontal direction, it also works wonders in damping down the boat's surging tendencies.

If you still aren't happy with the situation, or if you haven't been able to organize a weight, you must lay out a second anchor. This should be as large as is reasonably possible and should be shackled to a long, nylon rode with a short (9-foot) length of chain next to the anchor to guard against chafe on the sea-bed. The anchor (known as a *kedge*) should be laid on the greatest achievable scope, and in such a direction from the yacht that when she is lying head-to-wind, the two cables will make an angle of between 30 and 45 degrees at her bow.

If you have a good dinghy, the best way to lay out the kedge is to hook it over the stern and row away with it, while a foredeck hand pays out the line (rode) from the yacht. When you've maneuvered the dinghy into the desired position, heave the hook over the side. There'll be no sympathy for anyone foolish enough to let go the anchor without checking at least three times that it is clear to drop, and that no one in the tender has a bight of cable around any anatomical appendage. (Cables prefer feet and ankles, and no victim has ever returned to complain personally.)

When conditions are judged to be too tough for boat work, it is usually possible to motor the yacht up to the chosen spot for letting go the second anchor, gathering slack on the bower cable on the way if necessary, but in any case making certain that the propeller is not fouled. The job can even be done under sail in some circumstances.

Once the two anchors are set, the load should be evened out

between them so that as the nylon kedge rode stretches, it is relieved by the increasing mass of the weighted bower cable rising up from the bottom, and vice versa. The boat will ride much more quietly like this, and the increase in security is a mighty leap. Yachts have survived the most savage onslaughts imaginable by making arrangements of this sort.

## Anchoring Under Sail

The same wind and tide considerations apply to anchoring as to mooring. When you have chosen your spot and are planning your approach, you should ask the usual question, "Will my mainsail spill wind if required while I am going through the whole of this maneuver?" If the answer is "No," or if you are in doubt, drop the sail, and anchor under jib only.

### HEAD-TO-WIND ANCHORING

When there is no current, or if the wind and tide are running together, you will probably opt to keep your mainsail up until the

Wind against tide anchoring.

1. Mainsail is dropped on approach.

2. Boat speed is controlled so that when anchor is dropped boat is stationary over the ground (but moving ahead through the water.)

3. All wind is spilled from the jib (or it is rolled away, or dropped) so that, still moving ahead, boat moves back from anchor, laying cable as she goes.

4. When scope is run, cable is snubbed, anchor dug in, and sails dropped.

anchor is set. If you do, the only problem you may experience is that as soon as way is off the boat, her head will try to blow off the wind. If your yacht has a shallow forefoot, she may swing around so far that the main will no longer spill wind, causing the boat to sail around embarrassingly. If she habitually does this, it could well pay you to drop all your sails as you anchor, and allow the momentum of the boat blowing to leeward to dig in the pick when the end of the scope is reached. In the unlikely event of the anchor failing to take, you will be left somewhat legless, but in the sort of light boat where this tactic may be required, it will cause but little inconvenience to drag some sail back up again for another try.

## WIND AGAINST TIDE

Once the mainsail is stowed, these circumstances should cause no difficulty, so long as there is plenty of tide. With the yacht stemming the stream and the anchor cable being payed out, the jibsheet (or better still, the furling line, if you have one) is used as a throttle to allow speed through the water to be less than that of the tide over the ground. The cable can be laid out in a straight line, and the momentum of the boat going down-tide will be enough to set the anchor. Furthermore, you'll have no doubts that the anchor is holding as the water begins to flow past the boat like a river. If the wind is strong and the tide is not, it is difficult to be sure that your anchor has taken, so a careful watch will be needed until the turn of the tide.

## DIGGING IN THE ANCHOR UNDER SAIL

When under sail alone, the ideal way to dig in your anchor is to let the tide do the job for you. If there is no current running, you have two choices: either you let the boat blow off until you've run out your scope, then snub the cable and hope for the best; or you sail the anchor in. If you go for the former tactic, all will usually be well in strong winds, where the windage of the yacht will supply the necessary momentum. In lighter going, you'll need to opt for the active, latter approach if you want to be certain. These are the two main ways of digging in an anchor.

**Making a sternboard.** Here, the anchor is dropped head-to-wind with the mainsail set. The main boom (or better still, the mizzen, if available) is "backed" by physically pushing it out till it is running athwartships, and the yacht is sailing astern. With practice, and a little help from the people on the foredeck who can keep her head up by judicious control of the running cable, the boat can then be steered at a good-enough speed to really feel the anchor go "in." The ranges will stop opening, as the boat comes to rest; then they'll run back again as she bounces forward on her cable. In a boat well suited to the maneuver, this is probably the tidiest way of achieving the desired result under sail. It does, however, need to be tried a few times in a place where there is no audience. The initial period as the yacht begins to gather sternway makes for some awkward moments for the inexperienced helmsman.

**Anchoring downwind.** In this alternative method, the mainsail is stowed and the boat sailed slowly downwind under her headsail only. As she passes her chosen spot, the anchor is let go. Cable is run out as she sails away. When it is snubbed, the boat will quickly dig in her anchor, and you'll be left in no doubt that it's holding, because the boat will spin on her heel and lie head-to-wind with the headsail flogging its heart out. Once again, the yacht with a roller headsail is

Digging in the anchor under sail - no tide

WIND

1. Close-reaching approach - jib is dropped now.

2. Luff up and drop anchor.

3. Push boom out as far as possible so mainsail fills 'aback'. Steer away downwind, laying cable in the process.

4. Release main after snubbing cable and digging in the anchor.

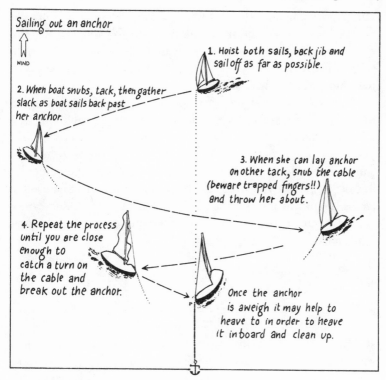

Sailing out an anchor

WIND

1. Hoist both sails, back jib and sail off as far as possible.

2. When boat snubs, tack, then gather slack as boat sails back past her anchor.

3. When she can lay anchor on other tack, snub the cable (beware trapped fingers!!) and throw her about.

4. Repeat the process until you are close enough to catch a turn on the cable and break out the anchor.

Once the anchor is aweigh it may help to heave to in order to heave it inboard and clean up.

at a distinct advantage when it comes to performing this operation cleanly.

## Weighing Anchor

Having taken such pains to dig the anchor in, you may, in due course, have to face up to the joys of pulling it out again when either the windlass (if you have one) or the foredeck crew (if you haven't) are unable to shift it. Under power, this presents no problem. Just shorten up until the cable is up-and-down, then run the engine hard astern. If that doesn't work, give back some cable and take a gallop at it full ahead. You'll then be exerting the power of the engine, plus whatever momentum the boat has managed to build up. When the anchor is not fouled, this will prove an irresistible combination. If it still won't give in, you may safely deduce that it is fouled. There is then little else to do but put on the kettle, consult the manual of seamanship, or call a diver.

If you're under sail and you don't have the strength or power available to trip the anchor, you will either have to pull it out with a headsail halyard led to a tackle or to your biggest sheet-winch, or you must "sail it out." This is done by tacking up to the anchor, shortening cable at each board until you sail across the anchor on a short scope. As you do, the cable is snubbed and the anchor is almost bound to give up the struggle and trip out. Great care is needed on the foredeck while this is happening, especially if the cable is all chain.

There are no special awards for working out why this should be.

## Kedging

When you are sailing a longish coastal passage in an area where tides run hard, it sometimes becomes advantageous to anchor during the periods of foul tide, especially when you are trying to work to windward in light airs.

A cruiser beating to windward at 3½ knots of water speed will have a Vmg (velocity made good to windward) of about 2 knots. In a fair tide of 2½ knots, this represents 4½ miles made good in an hour. Once the tide turns foul, however, progress is reduced to zero or worse if you have no engine, or are disinclined to make use of the one you have.

If the water is reasonably calm, it now makes all the sense in the world to anchor or, as it is called in these circumstances, to *kedge*. Using the boat's lighter anchor for convenience, it is often possible to kedge in water far too deep for the best bower and its chain cable. Tie all the available rope together, then bend this conglomeration onto the end of the official kedge rode, and the depth in which a well-equipped cruiser can kedge is astonishing. Racing yachts have been known to do it in 35 fathoms of water by using all their spinnaker sheets, guys, kedge warps, dock lines, genoa sheets, etc. The biggest problem at such depths becomes the friction of the water running past the kedge rode itself, but it's always worth a try if you are losing ground and cannot fetch an anchorage where the depths are more readily dealt with. If your kedge drags, remember, nothing is lost but a few miles made good.

## Mooring Stern-To

In certain parts of the world, mooring stern-to with the bow held off by a well-laid anchor is the normal way of berthing. This method is popular in the crowded harbors of the Mediterranean and in Scandinavia, where steep-to-rocky shores encourage one to berth as close in as possible. In the Caribbean, the technique is used in places such as the Pitons at St. Lucia.

The essence of the operation is to establish which berth you will

Stern-to mooring

This yacht has a right-handed propeller. She allows for this as she drops her anchor well out at 1. She then moves into the dock with her prop-walk pulling her into line, 2. At 3, once her quarter lines are secured, she can harden up her cable to lie sweetly in her berth.

enter, then set your anchor in a position at right angles to the side of the wharf. The wharf is approached by going astern until you are close enough to send two quarter lines ashore; once these are secured, the cable is shortened up so that the yacht is held at the desired distance from the wharf. If you favor a gangplank or *passerelle,* it can now be rigged so that you may step ashore in splendor. The only other options are the dinghy, the tightrope, the long jump, or mooring too close for comfort.

There are one or two points to note about mooring stern-to. The first is that because the pull on the anchor may not always come in a straight line (in a crosswind, for example), it must be allowed the maximum possible scope. If the harbor is crowded, it is important that you use chain cable. The chaos that would result from a small port crisscrossed with taut anchor rodes is easy to imagine and vile to contemplate.

If your boat is difficult to steer astern, make sure that you give careful thought to the question of her natural tendencies before laying your anchor. Failure to do this may leave you embarrassed athwart the hawse of what could have been a friendly neighbor. You may find, however, that careful use of the windlass brake and clear liaison between helm and winch-man will help to keep an otherwise headstrong yacht under tight control as she drops into her berth. Beware, though: Shame awaits the mate who snubs the cable completely before he is told. Once this happens in a cross-wind, all is lost, and the only remedy is to weigh anchor, fire the mate, and start all over again.

If you anticipate a strong blow from one side or the other, either lay your original anchor in that direction, or row out another anchor somewhat to windward in order to relieve the strain.

**Fouled anchors** are a common menace where mooring stern-to is the regular practice. If you discover someone else's gear over either your cable or your anchor itself, the solution is generally to make fast the end of a short line somewhere on your foredeck, lead the other end under the bight of the foreign cable, and lift it (either by main force or by winching) so that it comes clear of your own. Your anchor will heave up sweetly on nine occasions out of ten.

Where a number of large yachts have all laid out a pair of anchors in a tight harbor, trouble is guaranteed, and the results can be most gratifying to the uninvolved observer with a well-developed sense of mischief.

## Mooring Bow-To

This is, to all intents and purposes, the same as mooring stern-to, except that this maneuver is far easier to execute. The boat approaches the wall gently and at right angles. At the appropriate moment, the kedge is let go from the stern. Its rode, which must be carefully flaked out beforehand, is allowed to run. When the boat is far enough from the anchor to have laid a good scope, the rode is gently snubbed against her momentum, taking care not to actually bring her to a control-sapping standstill. This digs in the kedge far more securely than any amount of subsequent heaving and grunting.

Mooring bow-to has the additional advantage that, since most yachts draw more water under their sterns than under their bows, its benefits can be enjoyed where depths are less advantageous than those required for the stern-to equivalent. A less obvious "plus" is that with the boat bow-on to the dock, nosy passers-by are unable to check out what you are having for dinner.

# 12 OPERATING IN TIDAL RIVERS AND TIGHT HARBORS

It is a delight to work into a river at the end of a rough passage. The sea goes down instantly, and the wind generally eases as the boat travels farther inland. Crews relax, beer cans are popped, and before you know it, the poor old yacht is more vulnerable than she has been all the way across the briny deep.

Most navigable rivers are full to the banks with things to hit, and if you find a river that isn't, it is probably off the chart and abounding with shoals. Fortunately for us, all that is required to avoid these unpleasantnesses is concentration, and an awareness of the sort of places where they may lie. Sailing in rivers is far more fun than hammering about in the open. There is more to see, more to do, and there are no waves to spoil it all. It's a shame to see a handy cruising yacht drop her sails and start the diesel just because she has to make a few short tacks. Today's sailing boats are more capable of delivering the goods in this respect than anything the world has yet seen. They offer the competent boat handler a unique opportunity of achieving what we are all out there for: the satisfaction that attends the completion of a job well done.

Whether sailing or under power, there are one or two rules that are of great importance in keeping out of trouble's way during a bout of river navigation. These become axiomatic when, as is usually the case, there is a current running.

## WATCH RANGES CONSTANTLY

Any buoy, piling, branch, drying rock, anchored vessel, vessel under-way, or anything else in the water is a potential collision, whether you are headed for it or not. Regardless of where you think you are steering, the whole body of water is moving inexorably along. In a river, more than anywhere, you are at risk of being set into an object you fancy you are clearing.

Sighting ranges is never a problem in a river because there are always plenty of conspicuous trees, factory walls, lamp posts, cottage corners, and other salient items from which to make your selection. If the "target" is moving relative to the background, then at least you are not going to hit it with your own head. Bear in mind that you are not sighting ranges from the bow and the stern of your ship, but from wherever your eye happens to be. Whether the whole of your boat will clear the danger will remain a question of judgment.

Your boat's masthead is a classic weapon with which to chastise an obstacle. Many an unwary mariner has been brought up short as his radio antenna smashed against the top-mark of a navigation pile.

Transits in tidal rivers

strong tide

Boat A may be steering to miss boat B, but if the beast remains in transit with her bow, a collision is inevitable as the tide sets boat A down onto her.

Even more embarrassed is the skipper whose tricolor light hooks the masthead gear of a moored yacht, particularly if her owner is enjoying a quiet cup of tea in his cockpit at the time. You cannot judge accurately where your masthead will end up, so take no chances with it.

Watch out always for movement of the masts of other vessels. If you are approaching a marina, one mast creeping around among the forest may indicate that a fresh obstruction to your safe passage is about to pop out.

## DON'T BUNCH UP

Boats that bunch up together are a frequent nuisance late on sunny Sunday afternoons in popular yachting venues. Every boater in the area converges on the landfall buoy at 1600, bent on being away in the car by sunset. The motivation for this is clearly a desire to beat the traffic jam of yachtsmen rushing home to the dubious reality of Sunday evening TV, and the office the following morning. The result is a different sort of traffic jam in the river, but one which bears an annually increasing resemblance to the sort of nonsense we now suffer on the highways.

At the front, Joe Soap is toddling along at 4 knots, enjoying the peace. Coming up astern of him at or discreetly above the maximum permitted speed surge a variety of vessels under power. They all bunch into a gaggle which leaves none of them any of that vital commodity, contingency space. One unexpected incident can turn the procession into a pile-up. Add to this mix the depressing ingredient of the inevitable Human Mistake who is too important to obey the rules and who comes barging through the flock at 5 knots, pulling his wave behind him. Now you have a reliable recipe for extra insurance business.

Don't involve yourself. Stay away from Tunnel-Vision Terence, and the bejeweled popinjay with the "Turbo" stickers. You don't need these people. Let them squeeze one another out. Being in that much of a hurry has nothing to do with boating. If you let them, sooner or later they'll jam you into a position from which not even the snappiest seaman afloat could extricate himself.

## LOOK ASTERN

Keep a sharp lookout astern as well as ahead, especially if you are taking things gently. If another vessel is wanting to overtake, give her as much room as you safely can, and don't hesitate to slow down so that she can clear your path more quickly. There is a natural tendency among yachtsmen to set the throttle to the position that seems to suit the needs of the hour and then leave it where it is, come hell or high water. I cannot offer an explanation for this, but we all do it. It costs nothing to slow down for a minute or so, and two boats in line abreast take up four times as much room as one. . . .

# River Sailing

## CHOICE OF SAILS

Despite any urge you may have to go fast, when navigating in a river it is more important to see where you are going. You should, of course, be carrying enough sail to control the boat, but not so much that decisions are forced upon you more quickly than you might wish. Deck-scraping genoas are definitely out. You need a high-cut jib, ideally with a long hoist for good lift characteristics, but no deep overlap. The high clew will ensure forward vision for the helmsman, and the shallowness of the sail from luff to leech will make life easy for the crew if there is any short tacking to be done.

## TACTICS

If there are no constraints to the contrary (such as other vessels underway), the windward side of a river is the favored choice, particularly if the wind is forward of the beam. Wind direction becomes unstable as you travel farther inland. Having the breadth of the river

*Tacking through obstacles in a current*

Boat A is tacking up·river with the tide: B is on a steady bearing.
If she bears away, she will be trying to pass up·tide of B and may be set into her...

...much safer would
be to luff and let the tide carry her past the danger. She
will have enough way on later to bear away and begin sailing again.

"in hand" to windward may make all the difference if you are un-
expectedly headed.

## WORKING TO WINDWARD

Here, most of all, it is vital to keep an eye on your ranges if streams
are running hard. Suppose, for example, you are doubtful about
whether you will clear a moored vessel on this tack. The tide is setting you up nicely, but even so, you are unsure. Perhaps coming
about looks inconvenient. You are then left with two choices: either
you bear away, or you luff up. If luffing will put the tide more behind
you, it is probably the right thing to do, because you will then pass
on the down-tide (safe) side of the obstruction. Bearing away might
have been the answer if there were no tide running, but to bear away
onto the up-tide (dangerous) side of the moored vessel could leave
you open to the classic mistake of being set down onto it.

Always think at least two tacks ahead. This is not easy to do, but
failure to do it may place you in a blind alley, whereas a modicum of

foresight could have kept you clear, perhaps by coming about early, on a previous tack.

## LEE-BOWING

If you are working to windward in a foul tide and you are almost able to make the course up a stretch of river with your sails well full, great dividends are available if you are prepared to "pinch" just a little. Persuade your boat to present her lee rather than her weather bow to the tide, and she will be pressed to windward rather than being shoved down the proverbial tube. This will enable her to make the stretch in one tack. Even if the high pointing has slowed her down a trifle, and marginally increased her leeway, her gains will more than offset these minor losses.

As a matter of fact, once the tide is on your lee bow, the apparent wind will be slightly freed, which may just make all the difference. The reason for this is that if conditions were absolutely calm and the yacht were pushed sideways, she would feel an apparent wind in the

Lee-bowing in a river

tide

tide

wind

If a boat can contrive (by pinching slightly, if necessary) to lay her lee bow onto the tide, she will be lifted bodily to windward.
  A tide on the weather bow, even only slightly, will have the opposite effect.

opposite direction to that in which she was being propelled. When she is lee-bowed, she is pushed to windward. She must therefore experience a component of her "apparent wind mixture" from her weather side. This will inevitably be from farther aft than the main body of the apparent wind that would otherwise be blowing, and it will therefore have the effect of pulling the whole breeze a degree or two farther from the bow.

## TACKING

The importance of efficient tacking increases in direct proportion to the number of times a boat is to be put about in a given distance. At sea, 10 yards lost because the boat is allowed to stall will not be a hanging matter; 10 yards in a couple of miles is not much by any standards. In a river 100 yards wide, however, 10 yards given away or each tack may be a serious business, so make sure that you do not sag off while the jib is being winched in. Keep way on, steer high until the jib is setting on the new tack, and you'll slice up the river in a series of powerful boards instead of a shambling, hesitant worm-track.

**Huffling,** or the "Gravesend Hitch," as Thames bargemen used to call it, is a specialized form of tacking used only in rivers. It is useful in a foul tide for making ground along the edges of the navigable water where the stream is slacker. The boat must be moving well, but instead of being thrown smartly through "stays," she is held head-to-wind in order to carry her way as far as possible before filling on the new tack. Care is needed not to lose so much way that a stall is inevitable as the jib fills. This is a skill that requires some practice, but its acquisition will certainly repay your trouble.

Huffling works in rivers because the water is flat and the yacht can carry her way unhindered. At sea, it is not an effective technique because the waves will rapidly knock the boat to a standstill. In any case, as we have seen, a gain of 10 yards in a couple of miles out there, even if it were available, is hardly of measurable importance.

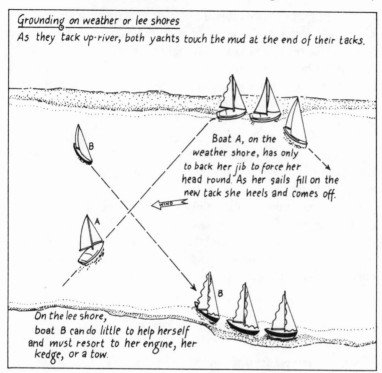

Grounding on weather or lee shores

As they tack up-river, both yachts touch the mud at the end of their tacks.

Boat A, on the weather shore, has only to back her jib to force her head round. As her sails fill on the new tack she heels and comes off.

WIND

On the lee shore, boat B can do little to help herself and must resort to her engine, her kedge, or a tow.

## GROUNDING

Of all the circumstances you could select in which to run aground, the most likely one is when you are tacking in a river. The temptation to go too close to the bank is often irresistible.

So long as you do it at the right time and not the wrong one, grounding like this is no cause for alarm or despondency. No damage will be done, and some respected sailors hold the view that if you don't "touch" every so often, you are not trying hard enough!

There are two rules about grounding on a muddy bottom:

- Never go aground on a falling tide.
- Never go aground on a lee shore.

The instant reaction, if you feel your boat touch at the end of a tack, must be to jam the helm down. It is of paramount importance to swing the boat's head through the wind before she loses way. As soon as her head is into the wind's eye, you can back the jib, which should finish off the job of pushing her around. Once she has filled on the new tack, heeling will do the rest, and nine times out of ten you will sail off.

If you don't manage to get through the wind, you may elect to risk bearing off and jibing around, which involves running to leeward with your keel in touch with the mud—highly undesirable. Otherwise, you must start your engine or lay out a kedge with which to pull your head around, doing all you can to heel the boat artificially at the same time. Of the three options, starting the engine is usually the popular favorite—though whether you go ahead, gritting your teeth, or astern, looking for the groove you just dug, is a question only your personal chemistry can decide.

## River Moorings

Moorings in rivers are often of the fore-and-aft, or "trot," type, taking the form of either pilings or buoys. Both sometimes cause problems for the unpracticed skipper, but the greater source of grief is undoubtedly the pilings.

Picking up a pair of empty pilings is actually quite easy, but people almost invariably chicken out of the job if there is another pair close by, already tenanted. They go and tie up to the luckless first-comer; then, if they are well-mannered, they pump up the dinghy and run out their own lines to the pilings.

It is simpler in the long run to approach the trot up-tide and lie briefly alongside the down-tide piling while a crewman *forward of your pivot point* attaches a rope to the piling ring (a round turn and a long bowline is the preferred method). Once the line is fast, you can motor on to the up-tide piling, paying out this first rope as you go. The bow is now laid alongside the up-tide piling, and the helmsman

Pile moorings

1. Boat approaches down-tide pile, stops, and attaches stern line — Always approach from LEEWARD.

2. Boat motors up-tide to second pile, paying out stern line as she goes.

3. Lee bow is laid alongside up-tide pile while bow line is attached. Once this is done the lines can be evened up.

maintains station with helm and throttle while the crew hitch up to it. All that then remains is to even up the lines.

Some people prefer to double their lines back as slip-ropes rather than tie up "permanently" to the pilings. If you aren't stopping long, there is much to be said for this. It's easier to leave when the time comes if both your lines are ready for instant release.

If the tide has turned, however, you might want to *wind ship* (turn around) before leaving, in which case the doubled lines will be a nuisance. Another problem a doubled stern-line frequently causes is that you overestimate its length and run out of rope before you arrive at the up-tide piling. One result of this is a frenzied rush to bend yet another jibsheet to the bitter end, with Cousin Misabel fumbling her double sheet bend in the heat of the moment and kicking the whole wretched tangle into the propeller. The other is that everyone stands about looking helpless while the yacht, securely tethered by the stern, drifts down athwart the tide in disarray.

Slip-ropes are useful, but not on every occasion, and it must never be forgotten that a slip-rope is highly prone to chafe if left overnight.

# 13

## DOCKING LINES AND FENDERS

It is a never-ending source of amusement to loll on a bollard near a favorite maritime watering hole and discreetly watch the yachts tying up to the dock. You can always tell the competent people. They know what they are going to do and they do it quickly, neatly, and with a minimum of shouting. Then they walk away, totally confident that the boat will not misbehave herself in their absence.

The other crews seem to leap around like monkeys in a circus act. They peer through fairleads as though sighting a competition rifle; they lead arbitrarily selected lines back as unnecessary slip-ropes; each line is made fast with a couple of half-hitches jammed up tight on the cleat or bollard; orders are bellowed concerning such apocryphal items as "back springs" (another circus act?); and, finally, the *pièce de résistance,* the spaghetti lying around on the dock is coiled down and laid alongside the bollards—the certain pointer to the fact that this crew has not been properly brought up.

The reason for the discrepancy in performance is not hard to find. It's back to the marina again. Marina berths are such a forgiving milieu that you can get away with any old cobble-up that more or less stops the boat from hitting either end or floating off altogether. The floats, or floating docks, are a convenient height for yachts, they are made of timber, they have an abundance of meaty cleats in handy places, and, because they float, *a yacht tied up to them is unaffected by the tides.* Most modern yachtsmen have "learned" their tying-up at marina berths.

Now compare docking against a real, live wharf or harbor wall in the west of Ireland, northern Brittany, southwest England, or Maine. Even a quayside in the virtually tideless West Indies will probably be made of old stone blocks (if you're lucky!) studded with gelcoat-munching bolt-heads, and will very likely be exposed to a 25-knot tradewind. What a difference! Take a liberty with your lines and fenders in any of those places, and you're in for expense, aggravation, or even a night spent hanging 25 feet above the sea.

Even if you never intend to tie up to anything other than an expensive floating dock, however, it is still worth doing the job right. It is quicker, neater, safer—and, for all those reasons, it's more seamanlike.

## The Classic Tie-Up

A well-tied-up boat has four lines on her: a bow line, a stern spring, a stern line, and a bow spring. The purpose of these lines is to secure the boat in such a way that she can't move significantly forward or aft, and that she remains snugly parallel to the dock. In order to see how the four lines working together achieve this, let's take a look at what each one would do individually.

**The bow line** secures the bow to the dock. It also prevents the boat from·moving astern, but if she tries to do so, this line acting alone will always snub her bow in to the dock.

The classic, four-line tie·up

bow line          bow spring      stern spring      stern line

The stern spring

If a boat is forced against her stern-spring and she has no other line rigged, she will pivot as shown. A bow spring acting on its own will have the opposite effect.

pivot point

wind or tide

The pair of lines

So long as the boat is being pressed astern, the bow line and the stern spring will act in concert to maintain her parallel to the dock. If no other lines are on her, she is free to move in or out like one leg of a parallel ruler. The other leg is the dock.

**The stern spring** should run from a point well aft, and certainly from abaft the boat's pivot point. Like the bow line, it will prevent the boat from moving aft, but if the boat is driven astern against the stern spring alone, her head will be forced off the dock and her stern pinned inward.

These two lines acting together prevent any astern movement, but as the illustration makes clear, they also work to keep the boat parallel to the dock. The spring tries to send the bow out, but, at the same time, the bow line is trying to jam it in. The effect is perfect balance. So long as the force acting upon the boat is in the right direction (in this case, forcing her astern), the boat will swivel on the pair of lines like one arm of a parallel ruler, the other arm in this case being the dock.

**The stern line and the bow spring** form a second pair of lines which similarly check any tendency the boat may have to move ahead. So long as all these four lines are set up at equal tensions, the boat will sit "pretty."

## Great Tidal Ranges

If the boat is secured to a floating dock, her lines can be set up hard so that she remains tight against her fenders. However, if the dock to which she is tied up is subject to a large rise and fall of tide, the more length that can be given to all the lines in equal proportions, the farther the boat will be able to move up and down the face of the dock without the need to tend them. In extreme cases, however, the lines will still require attention from time to time. The boat can be helped to lie close to the dock by absorbing the slack with weights (e.g., five-gallon water containers) on two of her docking lines.

## Spring Lines as Aids to Maneuvering

It isn't always either convenient or even possible to simply shove a boat off a berth into which a hard breeze is holding her, especially if she is over a certain size. When this is the case, the fact that a boat forced aft against her stern spring tends to throw her bow off the dock (vice versa with the bow spring) is of tremendous value when you are leaving. For maximum effect, the stern spring should be led aboard right aft, and the bow spring as far forward as is practicable.

Springing off.

This boat is being 'sprung-off' by the bow-spring. Note that the jet of water against the rudder blade from the propeller plays an important part. The spring line must be attached to the boat well forward, and it does not do to forget the fenders!
If it is expedient to do so, the bow can be sprung off equally easily by going astern against the stern spring line, though in this case the position of the rudder will be irrelevant.

WIND

## SPRINGING THE BOW OFF

All lines are let go except for the stern spring. A fender is sited on the quarter, and the engine is run in reverse gear (if there is a tidal stream setting from bow to stern, the engine may not be required). When the bow is far enough off the dock, the spring is let go and the boat can be steered away from the dock.

## SPRINGING THE STERN OFF

The same system can be effectively employed with the bow spring. The only difference is that the boat will spring her stern off more readily if the rudder is turned as if to steer the boat's head "into" the dock. This is because the blast of water off the propeller will be deflected by the rudder, providing an athwartships component to its effort.

When springing off either bow or stern, it usually makes matters more convenient if you double back the spring line, so that it can be readily "let go" from on board. Don't forget that, if you've sprung your bow out, your stern will be hard against the dock when you start to go ahead. You will therefore need to pivot the stern off the dock for a second or two before allowing it to swing any farther in as you steer away into open water. This brief shimmy is achieved by applying a touch of "opposite helm," and it is rather like a football player's body swerve. Doing it is a sure mark of an able boatman.

## The Rope's Ends

Unless you are leaving a rope doubled back for some particular reason, the immutable rules for securing a vessel to a dock are: short ends ashore; bights made fast aboard; ends coiled down on deck; one line for one job; one cleat for each line.

The reasons for these are various:

- It leaves a boat looking tidy.
- Lines can be tended from on board. (Circumstances may arise which will make it inconvenient, or even impossible to reach the dock.)
- Burglars will not steal the ends of your lines.
- Drunks will not trip over them and start fights.
- If you don't stick to the one-line, one-job rule, sooner or later you'll end up with the bight running hard and fast between two cleats, totally immovable from either, except by judicious application of axe or hacksaw. What is more, you'll be driven stupid by always having to fiddle with two lines at once.
- The sailor who stuffs two lines on one cleat will always need the bottom one when the top one is under a heavy load.

If you are sailing short-handed, there will be times when the ideal state won't be achieved immediately, but before you consider the boat to be tied up, nothing else will do.

## Making Fast on the Dock

### BOLLARDS

The best and easiest way to secure to a bollard is to drop a bowline over it.

### RINGS

Ropes made fast to these must have a round turn to prevent chafe. Once that is on, you can use a bowline, if you are certain you won't have to release the line under load. If there's some doubt, two half hitches are preferable. For a bulletproof solution, you can make a fisherman's (or anchor) bend, then pass the tail through the lay of the standing part, but beware! This won't let go, but it may end up needing a marlinespike to undo it.

### CLEATS

When the cleat is on the dock, you can drop a bowline over it, or make the line fast as you would on board if you wish to retain the option of releasing it under load from either end.

## Making Fast On Board

### CLEATS

So long as the cleat is big enough, the way to make fast to it is with a round turn, properly led so that it will not lock up, followed by at least two whole figures of eight. There should then be no need for a "locking hitch." Some cleats are too small for this, and some modern ropes are so springy and slippery that they have been known to work their way off the cleat. If this seems a possibility, a *single* locking hitch may be used, *the right way around,* but NEVER without at least two figures of eight underneath it.

WINCH BARRELS AND SAMSON POSTS

By far the most satisfactory hitch to use here is the *tugboat hitch*. This is formed by making a round turn on the post or winch barrel, then passing a series of bights (or loops) of the working end under the standing part and over the bollard. At no time is a loop passed through itself, or any other loop, so the hitch can never lock up. Like all good belays, it relies only on friction for its effectiveness.

Generally speaking, whenever a rope that may have to take some serious weight is made fast, consideration must be given to its lead and to whether it could possibly lock up under any foreseeable or unforeseeable circumstances. If in doubt, think again, and you will enjoy a life free of trouble and care.

At no time should the slack of a mooring line be taken up by winding turns of the standing part over the cleat on which it has already been made fast. If the rope is subsequently loaded up, this practice will result in a terminal lock-up from which the only escape is an application of the bolt-croppers. Any crewman who commits this foul atrocity should have the price of a new line extracted from his beer money.

# The Dynamics of Securing Alongside

Bringing a vessel alongside is one of those facets of seamanship where communication between skipper and crew is vital. It begins with a simple, unambiguous order which tells them all they need to know.

For example: "Starboard-side to. Bow line and stern spring first, please." (The two following chapters will explain why the skipper might have opted for those particular lines.)

The crew should now arrange their fenders at a suitable height on the starboard side (keeping one in hand, always, as a roving fender to be used when required). All four lines are led ready for action, with the two that the skipper has asked for in hand. Each line should be freshly coiled, or "flaked," for sure running.

Lines that are about to be taken ashore should have bowlines already made in them, if that's what is going to be used, and the crew should be standing with them at about *amidships* as the boat comes alongside. It is of no use to let the bowman hang over the pulpit. If the skipper does his job properly, the boat will end up alongside, not bow-in, so that the crew will be able to step ashore easily from amidships, or by the shrouds. They should take with them as much rope as they expect to need, then maybe half as much again, *and no more*. The bight of what remains is made fast aboard so that, if necessary, they can take a turn around a cleat or bollard on the dock to defuse an unhappy situation, should one develop. If all goes smoothly, they will merely drop their loops over the dock cleats, the slack will be taken up aboard and made fast, and that will be that. The other two lines are then run out, secured, dealt with in a similar fashion, and the job is done.

If the boat is sailing short-handed, you'll have to compromise this procedure by making fast at least one bight on the dock in the initial stages of the tying-up procedure, but it won't take more than a few seconds to regularize the situation once the heat is off.

## The Raft-Up

Where two or more yachts are tied up alongside each other, they should set springs between themselves, as well as bow and stern lines to the shore, or to the pilings if applicable. It is usually helpful if they also tie their bows and sterns directly to one another with short lines known as *breast lines;* but the most important thing is that by virtue of her shore lines or lines to pilings, each vessel is essentially carrying her own weight.

Cleats tend to be in short supply during raft-ups, so some intelligent lateral thinking may be required if seamanline standards are to be maintained.

Boats rafted up are safer if they are organized so that their masts do not coincide. If this is not done, a sea rolling in, or a heavy wash may result in spreader damage as the boats roll together.

Unorthodox tie-ups

Boats can be successfully tied up in all sorts of unlikely situations by referring to first principles. Here, the problem of keeping the stern 'in' has been solved by keeping the bow 'out' instead.

Note the starboard bow line.

## Unorthodox Tie-Ups

Occasionally a dock offers something short of the arrangements we would like to see. An example is the short slip in the illustration. Unless extremes of wind and weather are anticipated, this need not be a cause for gloom, so long as the basic principles of "which ropes do what" are considered. Frequently, an extra bow or stern line running off to some point on the side of the boat away from the slip is all that is required to achieve the desired balance.

# 14 DOCKING UNDER POWER

"Berthing under power? Easy as falling off a log!" seems to be the general assumption. Well, it can be. Yet one sees more disasters as yachts try to attach themselves to the dock, than in any other item on the general syllabus of seamanship.

In the previous chapter we have neutralized the problems that often stem from poor line handling. So long as all hands are well briefed on the expected sequence of events, the crew should perform as a smooth, well-structured team. That is half the battle. The other half lies entirely in the skipper's hands. There is no delegation when it comes to placing the yacht sweetly alongside a berth and holding her there while the line-men step ashore.

There are various sets of circumstances under which, from time to time, boats have to come alongside. As we look at some of them, you'll note that the principles of success are mere applications of the rudiments of boat handling we have already discussed. There will be times when combinations of forces not considered here govern the day, but this matters not a jot. Stand off and think about what is going to happen to the boat as you go in to the dock. Work out a plan, brief your crew, then go forward boldly.

## Berthing in Slack Water

If there is no tide running, the only elemental factor to consider in planning your campaign will be the wind. If there is no wind either, you will probably elect to dock on the side to which the propeller pulls your stern when you given the engine the "stopping burst." Thus, a boat with a right-hand propeller whose stern slides to port in reverse will opt for "port-side-to." That way she can approach the float or pier at an easy 30-degree angle. Just as her bow seems to be overhanging the dock, turn her hard to starboard and shift into reverse. She should pull herself neatly in so that she stops parallel to the dock.

If, for some reason, it is impossible to dock "with" the propeller, you should try to plan your strategy so that there is no need to run the engine in reverse at all. Come in very slowly at as shallow an angle as circumstances allow. If your boat displaces less than 10 tons or so, the crew will be able to man-handle her to a standstill. If she is heavier, they should be able to manage it by using the docking lines. Alternatively, you can tentatively "tickle" the motor in reverse after first warning the crew of what may happen, and making sure that they are ready with a line to keep the stern in.

## Strong Winds

Whenever there is a strong breeze blowing along a dock, you will normally elect to arrive upwind and let the wind take your way off, even if it means docking "against" the propeller.

If you are forced to come alongside downwind, this will present little problem so long as you are "correct-side-to." Thus, the left-handed boat will be able to drag her way off with the engine going in reverse while she prop-walks her starboard side in to the dock. So long as the crew are snappy with stern line and bow spring, all will be well. The other pair of lines can be put on at your leisure. If you are presented with this situation and no dock offers itself to your favorite side, that is a more serious matter altogether. This ugly prospect leaves you a poor selection of options. Either you go somewhere else, or you must come in as slowly as you can and get your crew ashore with bow spring and stern line before doing your best to help

The classic slack water approach

A. Approach dock at an angle of about 30°.

B. Go astern with engine (right-handed propeller pulls stern to port.

C. Boat prop-walks neatly alongside. Crew step off from shrouds with bow and stern lines.

Engine out of gear.

D. Lines ashore. Tidy-up.

Docking downwind against the propeller

This is to be avoided if possible. If you're stuck with it:

A. Approach dock at shallowest possible angle.

B. Crew steps off with line attached to boat imediately abaft her pivot point.

C. Crew takes a turn round bollard and brings on tension. Boat engine is now thrown astern. Between the two, the boat is brought under control.

them with the engine. These two magic ropes are now surged around the bollards (allowed to run under the control of one or more round turns) to stop you and to control your boat's natural tendency to poke her bow across the tow-path.

## THE SINGLE DOCKING LINE

Should you be faced with the above horror show with only yourself and one other crew, you'll have to use the single-controlling-line technique. It's not so good as the stern-line-and-bow-spring combo, but it will be the best you can do under the circumstances.

The line, which needs to be about one-and-a-half boat lengths long, is made fast to the rail (or led through a suitably placed fairlead) just abaft the pivot point of the vessel. While you are coming in to the dock *as slowly as possible,* your mate hops off with the rope and catches a turn around a cleat or bollard. He immediately starts surging, taking all the strain he can, short of snapping the rope. You help him by backing her down with the engine. With good teamwork, you'll win the day, but confidence and practice are needed. Except for the unfortunates with one of those impossible down-tide marina berths, the need to do this arises only rarely, for which we should all be truly thankful.

## STRONG CROSSWINDS

When there is a heavy breeze blowing *onto* the dock, the weight of wind will cause you to stall early and will blow your bow in to the dock as you take off way. You'll get there all right, but it won't be tidy.

You can avoid this by docking "with" the propeller and watching the bow carefully as you come in. Concentrate on the feel of the helm, and don't be afraid to approach rather faster than you otherwise would. You need a reliable gearbox for this; if yours is not, you should dock somewhere else, or be ready for the "bow-in shuffle." When you are almost at your berth, the boat is turned smartly to starboard, if you are coming port-side-to. How far she is asked to turn will depend on her discovered characteristics, but what you are

Docking in onshore winds

stern prop-
walks in

bow blows in

strong wind

Dock is approached fast enough to keep boat from stalling in cross-wind

Just before stopping her with a burst astern, the boat is swung off the wall. This is because as soon as she loses way her head will blow into the dock. Once the engine is running astern, her stern will 'walk' in, and her bow will blow in; the boat will then slide neatly sideways into her berth.

after is to get her into such a position that as way comes off, her bow will blow downwind at the same rate as the stern is prop-walking to leeward. This isn't so difficult as it sounds, and the boat should slot merrily into her berth. She'll be going sideways as she does, though, so plenty of fenders will be of the essence.

If the wind is blasting *away* from the dock, your problem is entirely different. The difficulty is not so much to plant at least some part of the yacht against the dock for a second or two, but rather that of persuading her to stay there long enough for the crew to organize themselves. A heavy-displacement vessel with high static lateral resistance (see Chapter 2) is far easier to deal with at a time like this than a lightweight flier, because she is less prone to stall and blow off at low speeds. The principle is the same for all boats, however, even if the execution varies in difficulty.

If you think there is a good chance of laying the shoulder of the boat alongside for enough time to allow your jumpers to hop ashore, you should dock with the propeller, keep as much way on as you dare for as long as you can, and be ready for the bow to blow away as you stop (brief your crew!). The lines ashore in this case should be a bow line and a stern spring. Once these are set, you can motor steadily astern against them. This will slide you back onto the dock if you've blown away from it. So long as you keep the power on, it will keep you there while the other two lines are made fast.

If the wind is coming off the dock at an angle somewhat abaft your beam, you will be better served by a bow spring and a stern line against which, of course, you will drive slowly ahead to enjoy the miracle of the parallel-ruler effect.

The use of lines and engine to pull in the boat under circumstances like these is infinitely more civilized than the application of groaning muscles. For a large yacht, it may be the only way.

If none of these techniques seems likely to work in your situation and your boat is light, you can always creep up to the wall bow-on, send your ship's monkey clambering ashore over the pulpit with a bow line, and worry about the details later as you try to drag the rest of the yacht bodily up to the wall.

## Docking in a Tide

With a few notable exceptions, tides usually run conveniently along a dock, rather than across it. In all but the most violent winds, this makes the decision about "which side to" an easy matter. Of course, you always dock head-up to the stream.

**Ranges** are of paramount importance while coming into a berth in a current. If you want to arrive with your cockpit alongside the point you've chosen, line up a cleat (or a crack in the dock, or a stationary frog) with a tree or road sign AND KEEP IT THERE. Then your approach is founded upon certainty, and nothing can go wrong.

**The slide.** Often, you are obliged to slot your boat into a gap only just long enough for her. As often as not, the space will be bounded forward and astern by expensive yachts.

The cross-tide slide

A. Boat is stopped over the ground but moving steadily through the water. Transit noted: bollard/pub door.

B. Boat is turned slightly so that she maintains station on her transit, but slides sideways (C, D) into her berth at E.

Now is the time to use the tide to its full potential. Instead of approaching the dock at your usual angle, run parallel to it until you are opposite the berth, then reduce your way until you are traveling at the same speed as the tide. At this point you will, of course, be stationary relative to the dock, but moving nicely through the water, with your rudder in full operation.

You now steer slightly in toward the berth (10 to 15 degrees is plenty), and the boat will begin to "slide" across. Watch your ranges, juggle your speed so as to keep them steady, and don't forget to straighten up into the tide as you arrive alongside. Keep steering, and keep your gears engaged while the crew set(s) up the bow line and the stern spring, then let the yacht settle back onto these while the other lines are run out.

A refinement on the "ranges" theme for this maneuver is to note two further pairs of objects: one ahead of your stationary, or cockpit range, and one astern of it. As you approach the berth, these should open in opposite directions while your central range remains "on."

Then there can be no possible doubt that you are sliding into the right place.

## THE DOWN-TIDE APPROACH

This is really the ultimate in incitement to catastrophe. It is only to be contemplated if there is no conceivable alternative, including abandoning the project completely.

You know the dangers. To spell them out would be superfluous.

Make sure you're coming in on your favored side. Go as slowly as you can through the water, which, remember, will add to your ground speed as it pours past the dock. Be ready with your stern line and bow spring (or single 'midship "stopper") and don't forget to turn your helm so as to point the rudder toward the dock as soon as you are stationary *relative to the ground*. You will by then, of course, be going astern through the water, and by dealing in this way with the rudder, you will be inducing the boat to tuck her stern in to the dock.

## THE DOWN-TIDE "DEAD END"

There is occasionally an unusual alternative to what seems to be an inevitable down-tide approach to a berth. Even if there is not enough room alongside, or down-tide of it to turn the boat around so as to make an up-tide approach, there may still be space up-tide to swing her. If this can be arranged, the problem is solved, so long as the tide is strong enough.

Once the boat has turned to face the stream, she will be stemming it under perfect control. You should now allow her boat speed to fall a fraction of a knot below the velocity of the tide, and she will drop steadily back over the ground toward the berth. When she is parallel to it, you have only to put her helm over gently, then power up the engine a fraction so as to raise her speed to that of the tide, and she will slide perfectly into her berth with a sigh of relief that her skipper is a creative artist.

# 15 DOCKING UNDER SAIL

Berthing alongside under sail is undoubtedly the apex of the sea-man's art. Performing the task well involves everything so far covered by this book, with the exception of one or two of the subtleties of power handling. The possible variations in wind and tide are endless, and it could be said that only the complete boat handler who is confidently at home with his command can promise a tidy result on all occasions. However, that shouldn't put you off coming alongside without using your engine when the circumstances are encouraging. A strong tide with the wind against it, for example, generally makes life easy if there is plenty of space at the dock.

When the chance arises, why not have a go? There are two good reasons why you should.

The first is that nothing satisfies like a complete passage made without recourse to the auxiliary power unit. To move one's vessel from one location to another using nothing but one's own skill and the winds of heaven is always a memorable experience. To have all but succeeded and then to "blow" the whole business because of an irrational fear of docking under sail, is sad indeed.

The second reason is that one day you're going to be forced to do it for real. When that happens, you may well have a number of other problems to add to your list, so you will feel a great deal more confident if you have berthed without power on a number of earlier occasions.

## Organization

A well-thought-out plan is the essence of arriving under sail. Consider any difficulties which may arise during the maneuver, such as critical wind shifts, movement of other boats, or sudden gusts of breeze. Then give thought to everything that can go wrong on deck, because otherwise something probably will. Is the mainsheet clear to run? Have you taken up the slack on the topping lift? Will the jib halyard foul up like it did two days ago? Most important of all, do your crew understand what's happening, why it's happening, and precisely what they are expected to do? Have they organized their docking lines and fenders? Is everyone clear as to who is to step ashore with the stern line, and whether he is to drop a bowline over the bollard on the dock, or surge the line to take off the last of your way?

## The Escape Route

We've already mentioned several times the implications of the fact that a sailing boat has no brakes. Now is when it really counts. Unless you are confident that absolutely nothing can go wrong with your scheme, you must leave a "chicken alley" down which you can escape for another try if the sequence of events fails to live up to your expectations. There is no shame in going around again.

## The Dead Loser

Some berths, on some occasions, will be impossible to enter directly under sail. To a certain extent, the decision about whether this is the case or not will depend upon your assessment of your own skill and judgment, but there are many setups that John Paul Jones himself would have taken one look at and sailed on by.

When you are confronted with one of these dead losers, you have two alternatives: either you forget the whole thing, or you anchor off and "warp in." If the berth lies to leeward of you, it should be possible to ease your cable until you drop into the berth; if it lies to windward, you will have to row a line ashore and then warp yourself up to the berth. In either case, there will be the advantage of an anchor laid out when it is time to leave. You will be able to let go all your lines and move out to the hook. Getting underway will then be a simple matter.

Liberal use of lines, or warps, was one of the ways seamen of old managed to maneuver their unwieldy vessels into tiny harbors. They thought nothing of it because they had no choice, and if we are ever to survive without engines, that is how we must think as well. There is no way in this world that a sailing vessel of any description at all can retrieve herself from a dock that is dead to lee without external assistance. Lay out an anchor, however, or run a line across to a buoy, and the job presents far fewer problems to the owner of a 40-foot fin-keeled yacht than it ever did to the nineteenth-century fisherman, heaving with muscles of iron to warp his 12-ton smack off the dock.

## Onshore Winds

If you are docking with a wind well forward of the beam but blowing onshore, you are faced with an extra factor when planning the maneuver. Especially if the breeze is strong or gusty, your sails are going to blow over the dock as you come in. If you are arriving outboard of another boat, they are going to blow over her as well, and either of these possibilities is undesirable. In the first place, your boom and the ironbound clew of your genoa might be spoiling somebody's paint, or braining a well-wisher on the wharf. More important, though, is the possibility that while you are still underway you will hook some static object with the bight of one of your sheets. This can be either embarrassing or expensive. It might well be both.

In general terms, this means that when the dock is to lee, you are better off without your mainsail, regardless of the tidal stream. The boat is trying to blow on anyway, so you are not exactly fighting to work up to weather. Most modern yachts sail adequately under genoa alone, and with careful timing you may be able to drop this as well, if not roll it away, just before you come up to the wharf. Even if you can't, at least you've only one flailing sheet to concern yourself about.

## Offshore Winds

### WIND FORWARD OF THE BEAM

When the wind is forward of the beam, particularly if the tide is running to leeward, you will have to keep your mainsail up and ready to draw until you are safely alongside with a bow line and a stern spring on the dock. This is because if the boat is allowed to lose way so that she develops lee helm and begins to stall, you won't regain control quickly enough unless you've plenty of power available from abaft the center of lateral resistance. Fortunately, if the wind is in this

Offshore wind forward of the beam

wind

tide

If you are docking in an offshore wind and the tide is running to leeward, it may be possible to slide in on a transit, controlling speed by spilling wind on a close reach, or even close hauled.

Offshore wind abaft the beam

wind

tide

The easiest docking of all. Mainsail stowed, speed controlled with jib sheet, or jib furling line. Tide must be running to windward, otherwise you wouldn't be docking downwind, so tide is used to control 'ground speed' to perfection.

direction you'll be either beating up to the berth or on a close reach, so spilling wind to dump unwanted drive will be an easy matter.

## WIND ABAFT THE BEAM

The only time you will be docking with an offshore wind abaft the beam is when the tide is running to windward along the wharf. The mainsail will be down, but there will be no problem working the boat up to the dock. You are not trying to punch her to windward, and you will have the tide on your lee bow. This places you in the perfect position. You can slide the boat sideways into her berth, just as you would under power. Instead of using the throttle to control your speed to equal that of the tide, you use the jibsheet. If you can't lose enough way because of the windage of the flogging sail, don't be afraid to drop it, then hold up a small portion of it if necessary. If it's a roller-furler, of course, the job is a complete delight.

This last circumstance is one in which it is literally as simple to dock under sail as it is under power. It's probably even safer, in fact, because you can't lose your drive at a crucial moment by kicking the dog's lead over the side and into the propeller.

## The Checking Line

Except in the most ideal of worlds, a yacht under sail is often carrying a little way as she comes alongside. The short line described in the previous chapter which leads from immediately abaft the pivot point of the boat is of great use here. Way can be taken off quickly and effectively by an able rope handler who steps off with this line and catches a turn around a strategically placed bollard. Once the boat has stopped moving, the rope can be shifted up to a cleat or bollard on the floating dock just opposite its fairlead on the rail, where it will hold her quietly while the other lines are organized.

## Fenders

It needs no imagination to see why plenty of decent fenders are required when sailing alongside. It often pays to site an extra one well forward, because if the boat is stopped by using her lines, she may find that her bow is "snubbed in." It shouldn't be your intention for this to happen, but in reality it often does. The roving fender is a lifesaver, too, on many occasions. Always keep it handy.

One of the greatest satisfactions yacht cruising affords is to complete a passage without ever having used the engine. Such a day may be challenging, but to see it through until the boat lies quietly tied up in a peaceful place is gratifying in the extreme. There's no need to try to achieve this every time you go out, but once in a while, when conditions make it feasible, such a resounding success will add another dimension to your seafaring. Satisfaction will deepen as another link is forged with the men who wrested a living from the sea under sail alone, and who must always be our inspiration.

# 16

## BOAT HANDLING IN ADVERSITY

Of the four topics considered in this final chapter, "man overboard" and "sailing after losing the rudder" are true emergencies. Handling a yacht offshore in heavy weather, and the occasional towing job are merely circumstances out of the ordinary where thought is required concerning the correct techniques to adopt.

## Man Overboard

Man-overboard recovery is a two-stage operation. The first stage concerns bringing the boat close to the casualty and stopping her there for long enough to be able to tackle the second stage, which is assisting him back on board.

Perhaps the most vital aspect of phase one is to ensure that contact with the casualty is never lost. Someone on board should be watching him the whole time. While never forgetting this essential point, there are a number of systems you can adopt for bringing a boat to rest close by, or even alongside, a crew member in the water. Which you opt for will depend on your boat, the conditions, and your assessment of your own competence. Here are three of the most effective methods.

### THE REACH-TURN-REACH

This tactic, which has already been discussed in Chapter 9, is arguably the best of all the systems, but it has two drawbacks. To be sure

Man overboard recovery:
The heave to method

As soon as the man goes overboard,
the boat is hove to as best as she may
be on the opposite tack. The boat does
not travel far from the victim, so a
line can be thrown to him, or the
boat manoeuvred closer with sheets
and tiller.

of pulling it off, boat handling of a high standard is required, and it involves taking the boat away from the casualty while working up the sea-room for the pickup approach. At night, especially if you are not certain that the victim has caught hold of the light you threw him (!), or if the light has failed yet again, the risk of losing touch with him in the dark may be considered too great. For all that, it is well worth taking the time to practice this system, particularly if you suffer from an unreliable engine, or one that will not deliver adequate punch to maneuver in heavy seas. You have more sail control using this method than any of the others.

## THE HEAVE-TO METHOD

This has the advantage of staying hard by the casualty at all times. As soon as the wretch goes "over the wall," you shove the helm down regardless of your point of sailing, bring the boat through the wind, and leave the jib aback. In theory, this will heave her to. In practice, it is sometimes a messy business, with bights of mainsheet garroting the cook as he leaps up the companionway to join the action, but sometimes it works beautifully. Once the boat has settled, you may find you are close enough to pass a line to the victim. If you can't manage this, it is often possible to work the boat across to him by juggling sheets and tiller.

## THE MOTORSAILING METHOD

While there is no doubt that the job of maneuvering to a swimmer is better tackled without resource to the engine, the motorsailing method will remain the hot favorite for skippers with serious doubts about their capacity to cope with either of the other two systems. It is also the best way to teach your inexperienced crew to handle the boat in the event of the ultimate horror—going overboard yourself.

While the casualty's position is watched at all times, the jib is dropped to the deck or rolled away. The boat is then allowed to fall downwind of the victim, and the engine is started *after first making absolutely sure that no rope of any description can find its way into the propeller.* The final approach is made from approximately dead

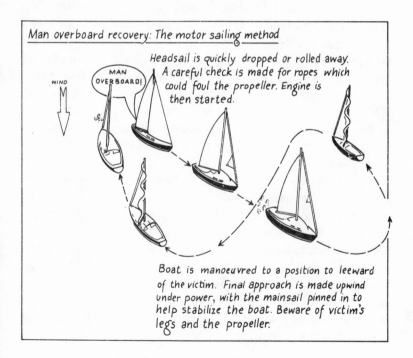

Man overboard recovery: The motor sailing method

MAN OVERBOARD!

WIND

Headsail is quickly dropped or rolled away. A careful check is made for ropes which could foul the propeller. Engine is then started.

Boat is manoeuvred to a position to leeward of the victim. Final approach is made upwind under power, with the mainsail pinned in to help stabilize the boat. Beware of victim's legs and the propeller.

downwind, with the mainsheet pinned in amidships. The sail will steady the boat, and the engine should give the required control. Never forget, though, that you have a propeller thrashing around down there which can inflict shocking injuries on a swimmer.

If you lose someone while you are running with a preventer on or a spinnaker set, the coolest deck work will be needed if the victim is not to disappear from view, possibly for ever. Work out in your mind what you would do if this were to happen, then try it, and make sure your plan is feasible.

Whichever method you adopt, always remember that if the casualty is conscious and still in reasonable condition, it is better to stop 5 yards from him and toss him a line than it is to risk injuring him by coming alongside him in a seaway.

It is also important that the helmsman does not lose sight of the casualty for even a few seconds toward the end of the final approach. This is particularly easily done if you are using the reach-turn-reach method and are intending to place the casualty on the lee side as you lose way. The problem is that if you allow this to happen, you are immediately at risk of running him down, which could well put a permanent end to his problems. What is more, from the point of view of the person in the water, the boat may then present her stem to him. This is demoralizing in the extreme, and what you are after from him is that he should remain calm and not give way to panic. Nothing is more likely to have the opposite effect than the sight of a 6-foot stem slicing toward him at 4 knots.

When the casualty is alongside, the next task is to hoist him aboard. In the absence of a boarding ladder, you might try lowering a bight of line into the water. The tail of the jibsheet is perfect for the job. The swimmer steps in this and, as the boat rolls, he raises himself up as best he can while helpers on deck take up the slack around a cockpit winch. After two or three "grunts," he will probably be high enough to roll under the top guardrail. The lower rail should be let go to make the job easier. It's a very fat person indeed who can't slither under the upper wire. To do so is a hundred times easier than trying to clamber over it.

If this does not work, you will have to devise a lifting arrangement using a halyard, a turning block, and a winch and/or a tackle (the boom vang, detached for the occasion, perhaps?). Every yacht should have a "crane" of some sort that can be put together from her own gear and perhaps one or two dedicated items carried for the purpose. Its use should be well rehearsed so that it can be deployed rapidly and surely at any time of day or night, should the need arise.

**Patent man-overboard equipment** developed in the 1980s has greatly improved the chances of both finding and recovering a crew member in the water. One such system is the "Seattle Sling." As soon as someone goes over the side, a buoyant lifting device that is attached to the yacht by 150 feet of floating line is thrown after him. The yacht circles the swimmer until the line is towed past him. Once in touch with the line, he can easily settle himself into the sling itself and be pulled alongside the yacht. (She must now, of course, be hove to.) Since the sling is similar to those used in helicopter rescues, the person in the water is in the best of all circumstances to be lifted aboard.

Another first-class development is the "Jon-buoy" type of lifesaving equipment, manufactured in the United Kingdom. The Jon-buoy is best described as a sort of mini-liferaft that is launched immediately upon losing a crew member over the side. The raft self-inflates and has a substantial integral drogue mechanism which keeps it stationary so that the swimmer can easily gain contact. Its comparatively large size and bright color make the Jon-buoy easy for the watchers to spot, while its design enables the swimmer to enter it without difficulty so as to await recovery. The raft also features a lifting sling. This system can be used in conjunction with personal radio beacons (EPIRBs) and automatic deployment arrangements which release the buoy as soon as anyone goes "over the wall." The Jon-buoy proved successful in the Southern Ocean during the Whitbread Round the World Race in 1989/90.

How successful you are in a rescue situation both at bringing the boat to the victim and at lifting him back on board will depend entirely upon how much practice you have given yourself. Man-overboard drills should be completely automatic so that when the moment comes, you snap into action like a well-serviced machine, rather than vacillating for those vital seconds that could make the difference between life and death.

## Coping with Rudder Loss

If your rudder jams hard over, you have real problems. Fortunately, it is more likely that you will lose the rudder altogether. If you are unlucky enough to suffer the latter, you will require a "jury" steering system to use in conjunction with a carefully balanced sail plan. What you devise will depend on the gear you have available, but there are two arrangements that can be made using equipment to be found on most modern yachts.

The spinnaker pole jury rudder

secure lashing to pulpit, allowing some lateral movement

spinnaker pole

control lines lead to winches

anchor, to keep business end down in the water

## THE SPINNAKER-POLE JURY RUDDER

The illustration is self-explanatory as far as rigging this is concerned. On a well-balanced boat, the drag of the pole alone may do the job, but if it proves inadequate, a dinghy paddle or a washboard lashed to it will help.

One of the problems usually experienced with spinnaker-pole rudders is that of keeping the business end down in the water once the yacht is underway. The anchor lashed to the pole assists in this, and the added drag may improve the effectiveness of the setup as a steering device.

The business of heaving the inboard end of the pole from side to side soon becomes tiring, and that is why the control lines are fitted. They have been found extremely helpful in many cases.

When a spade rudder is lost, the directional stability of the yacht will probably be so badly affected that this method won't work well, if at all. If so, you should try the bucket-and-pole method.

## THE BUCKET-AND-POLE METHOD

This looks fanciful, but it has been used successfully. You do need a proper bucket, however. Any item of lesser quality than the pre-war galvanized clanger will fail. That is a promise. If you don't have one, you'll have to contrive another means of supplying the necessary drag.

The system works by a controlled counter-action to the boat's natural tendency to round up to windward. The sails are set so that the yacht is trying hard to luff. The pole is arranged on the leeward side to encourage the drag of the bucket to counteract this. By winching the bucket inboard or outboard with the rope passing through the quarter-block, the degree of "helm" is varied to suit the pull of the rig, and maintain a straight course.

## THE SWIM-LADDER-STEP PINTLE

If your yacht has a straight-down transom or a retroussé (reverse counter) stern that is rigged with a boarding ladder, or "swim lad-

The bucket jury rudder

Yacht is rigged so she tends to round-up to windward.

Bucket is winched inboard or outboard from cockpit winch via block on stern. As it moves, the 'weather helm' it supplies is varied.

Spinnaker pole is guyed solidly

der," the brackets by which this is attached may well provide excellent points of attachment for the stock of a jury rudder. Such a rudder could be made from a booming-out pole with the head's door lashed and bolted to the lower end. In fact, exactly this has been used successfully on an 800-mile passage to safety.

The essence of coping with rudder loss is in meeting the challenge with the use of seamanlike initiative. It is rare indeed for there to be absolutely nothing that can be done.

# Towing

## APPROACHING A DISABLED VESSEL

If you are closing in on a disabled vessel not under command (out of control) with the intention of passing a tow line, you should pay attention to the fact that she will be drifting. Depending upon the nature of her disablement, she may be trailing all manner of impediments in the water, particularly to windward of her. These will catch your propeller if you give them half a chance—so, don't. Assess carefully the boat's rate of drift before you decide which way to approach her. If it's blowing hard and you come up from leeward, she may come down onto you before you realize what is happening. If you approach from windward, there will be the danger of fouling your propeller or of being blown down onto the casualty herself. It might well be that the safest thing to do is to position your own boat across the wind from the tow, coming up from downwind to do so.

Having come as close as you dare to the beneficiary of your efforts, you should pass your line to the boat's skipper or crew, or he should pass his. Which you opt for will be decided by your negotiations concerning any liability for salvage. If a disabled vessel takes the line offered by a towing vessel, she is accepting a *prima facie* duty to pay up. The line will be hove across or, if it is too heavy, a heaving line will be used, followed by the towing hawser. This should always be long enough to allow at least a couple of boat lengths between the two vessels, but if the sea is rough, the longer it can be, the better, because its length will damp down any snubbing tendencies. For this reason, too, nylon rope is to be preferred for its great strength and elasticity.

**The towing vessel** should arrange for the tow to be from the centerline of her stern, if at all possible. Tugboats use hooks sited above their pivot points in order to enable them to steer properly while towing. Yachts cannot enjoy such refinements because, amongst other things, the backstay may get in the way. If it does, rig a towing strop, made up of ordinary stout line, with one end on each quarter, and attach the tow line to its bight with a bowline.

It is important that either vessel can release the tow line if necessary. If you are towing on a strop, one end can be let go and the bowline will slip off, but however the tow line is secured, under no circumstances should a locking hitch be used, or a loop be allowed to take the strain. The line should be belayed so that no matter what the load, it can always be instantly let go.

The towing strop
Both ends of the strop are secured so that they can be released under load.

towing strop

bowline

to tow

**The towed vessel** should bring the tow line aboard securely over her bow. If she has no closed fairlead, the tow line will need to be tied into whatever other arrangement is made, with a knife kept at hand to cut it loose if need be. Chafe is the desperate enemy of tow lines, so steps should be taken to neutralize it. A length of plastic hose is best, but if this isn't convenient, plenty of heavy canvas or rags will serve for a limited period. If the loads are going to be excessive due to snubbing caused by the seaway, the tow line should be secured to several strong points and kept in tension. This can generally be arranged by "backing up" the foredeck cleats or bollards with the primary winches.

Alternatively, the tow line could be passed around the mast a couple of times before making fast on a sound cleat—provided, of course, that the mast is stepped on the keel. Securing to a deck-stepped mast would be asking for trouble in any but the calmest of conditions. The rope should never by physically tied to the mast. If it is, you'll not be able to let go once the weight comes on.

The towed boat should be steered at all times. Great care is needed when the strain is being taken up, because the pull may come in an unusual direction which will try to force the boat onto her beam ends, particularly if the towing vessel is powerful.

At all times before and during a tow, communication between the two vessels must be maintained.

# Heavy Weather

Sooner or later, most of us are faced with riding out a gale at sea. Sometimes we are far from land and there is no choice; on other occasions, shelter may be seductively close at hand, only to be discounted as being too dangerous to approach. There are various options open to a yacht caught out by stormy weather. Which tactic she chooses should depend on her sea-room, her crew strength, and on what sort of boat she is.

## HEAVING TO

This is an excellent option in tough conditions. Unfortunately, it only really works in yachts with the considerable wetted area that usually goes with heavy displacement. Such vessels also enjoy a deep forefoot, which will help them to point high in the hove-to state and to make a minimum of leeway. A 32-foot (overall length) boat of this type can heave to comfortably in wind strengths of Force 8 or 9 with an equivalent general sea state. If she is found to be making more leeway than is desirable, or if she is tending to lie beam-on to the seas, she can be encouraged to fore reach slowly by easing the headsail across, as far as the yacht's centerline if need be, though if it goes this far, it may help to bring the helm more amidships. At this point the boat will begin to sail (see Chapter 9), albeit slowly and with considerable leeway, but she will certainly be maintaining her overall windward position.

Heaving to is not an available hard-weather technique for a lightweight yacht with a fin-and-spade profile. She will not be stable when hove-to because her hull form leaves her prone to being knocked around by the waves. She will also make more than an acceptable amount of leeway as a result of her lack of static lateral resistance (see Chapter 2).

The semi-hove-to state

Some boats will work their way inefficiently but comfortably to windward without a helmsman if they are set up like this.
  Others may require a helping hand.

WIND

main eased from close-hauled position.

helm either free or being tended.

jib clew held amidships by both sheets.

## LYING A-HULL

When conditions become so heavy that the hove-to yacht is over-pressed even by her minimum canvas, one possibility is to take every-thing down and lie a-hull. For a boat with poor stability character-istics, this is very hazardous, but generally speaking, the sort of craft that heaves to satisfactorily in heavy seas will also be in good order to lie a-hull and will not make an outrageous amount of leeway while doing so. When a boat is lying a-hull, the helm should be lashed amidships. If you lash it "down" and the boat gathers way, she may round up into a wave, be knocked astern, and be brought up short on her rudder. Damage to the steering gear will almost certainly result.

The danger of lying a-hull is that because the boat lies beam-on to the seas for much of the time, the possibility of a knockdown must be considered. She should therefore be completely battened down, with everything properly secured both on deck and down below. It cannot be stressed too highly that for a light, flat-floored yacht in a steep, high sea, the probability of being flattened, or even rolled clean over, must never be discounted.

Both heaving to and lying a-hull have the advantage of requiring no effort from the crew. If you habitually sail short-handed and you want to be confident of taking really bad weather in your stride, there is much to be said for opting to sail a boat that can look after herself. Unfortunately, this usually means giving up some light-weather performance and in-harbor maneuverability; but then, as the philosopher said, "You can't have everything in this life."

## RUNNING OFF

Traditionally, this has been an odds-on favorite for well-crewed boats, for the sound reasons that it reduces the force of the seas and apparent wind, and keeps the boat end-on to the waves, lessening the chance of a knockdown.

The crux of safe running is to keep your speed down. Once a yacht's speed approaches, or even exceeds her theoretical maximum, she is in grave danger of broaching. It this happens to her in a steep sea, it is quite likely that the centrifugal force of her turning, coupled with the wind in her sails as she lies beam-on and aggravated by the next big wave, will combine to throw her down onto her beam ends or beyond.

Most boats steer easily at the equivalent of their best speed to windward, so you should choose your sail area to maintain something like this speed. If it really blows, you'll end up under bare poles—sooner rather than later, in a lighter boat. If you're still going too fast, you'll have to tow something astern to slow you down. Try long warps streamed in a bight. They work well, but they really must be *long*. Forty-foot docking lines aren't worth a cent (they aren't much good for tying up with, either).

In recent years, substantial progress has been made in the commercial development of the *drogue*. One of these devices can be towed with dramatic effect astern of a speeding yacht. Unlike the old-fashioned sea anchor, which was unwieldy, often unreliable, and always controversial, a modern drogue provides a sensible answer to a real problem which the comparatively flyweight modern cruiser has brought with her as one of the less desirable items in the package.

## SURFING

*For advanced drivers only, or the young in spirit.* If the weather is "going your way" and you are pressed for time or feeling in need of adventure, you may find that you are able to induce your boat to surf. We have discussed the safe way to run before a gale. This is an exciting alternative, but the penalties for making a mistake are high, as a broach may well be the result. A boat which broaches at speed in a big sea can end up on her beam ends, but for all that, it must be said that life offers few exhilarations to compare with the feeling you get as 15 tons of yacht takes off down the face of a 20-foot wave and goes roaring away at twice her theoretical hull speed.

The technique is easy enough, but it requires a sensitive seat to your pants: As you feel a steep one lifting the stern of the boat, luff her *carefully* about 15 degrees. Just before the crest arrives, bear off onto a dead run. If you have caught the wave, you'll be on your way, and you must now be ready for anything. The most likely event is that the boat will heel somewhat to windward, which will induce her to continue bearing away. If this tendency is not checked, a jibe-broach is the inevitable result. Firm application of lee helm at the right moment will, however, avert this horror. Once you feel the boat come upright again, hang on, and let her go. Just make sure you keep the shouts of "Geronimo" to a minimum, or you'll disturb the watch below, who are missing all the fun.

## SAILING TO WINDWARD

Although yachts of the new wave have proved less able than their predecessors to look after themselves, their pure sailing performance represents considerable progress. This fact can be used to their advantage in the form of one survival method that has been developed in recent years. Since the lightweight boat is unhappy presenting her beam to heavy seas, she must be kept bow- or stern-on. The latter is

Running off.

Depending on her
type and size, a boat will run first under reduced sail, then,
as conditions worsen, under bare poles. When it really blows
she may have to resort to towing warps, or even a drogue,
to keep her speed down.

served by running off, the former by working her to windward. If she
has a good suit of sails, a well-found modern cruiser/racer can be
sailed upwind under minimum canvas in very heavy going indeed.
She will need skillful steering to keep her sails just on the edge of
luffing, for if she is allowed to fall away beam-on at the wrong

moment, she may be knocked flat by wind and sea; but there are plenty of recorded instances of yachts coming unscathed through moderate and sometimes severe gales by successfully adopting this technique.

If the boat is not powerful enough to sail to windward, or her sails prove inadequate for the task (especially likely if she has a roller headsail), she may find she can make a working compromise by dropping her headsail, sheeting the deep-reefed main in flat, and motoring slowly ahead with the wind about 30 degrees on the bow. The mainsail will provide some drive and will steady her. The engine will do the rest.

Unlike every other aspect of sailing and boat handling, heavy-weather seamanship is not something that is open to frequent rehearsals, but if the principles of how a yacht moves through the water have been thoroughly understood, and the necessary skills for putting them into dynamic practice have been mastered, the rising gale will hold no terrors for the skipper of a well-found craft.

# INDEX